# Writing Short Stories, Plays and Poems:

## An Introduction to Creative Writing

by

Clarence Brown
Professor of English
Marquette University

E. J. Heiman
English Department Coordinator
Monona Grove High School
Monona Grove, Wisconsin

American Book Company
New York  Cincinnati  Atlanta  Dallas  San Francisco

Every reasonable effort has been made to trace owners of copyright materials in this book, but in some instances this has proven impossible.

The publisher will be glad to receive information leading to more complete acknowledgements in subsequent printings of the book, and in the meantime, extends apologies for any omissions.

*Photography and art by* Hunsberger from Monkmeyer (p. 142); James B. Johnson from DPI (p. 143); Grete Mannheim from DPI (p. 12); Universal Color Slide Co. (p. 19); Chi Chuan Wang (p. 145)

The American Book Writing Series was edited by Anne Marie Mueser, Associate Professor of Education, Teachers College Columbia University, and produced by AMM Productions Ltd.

AMERICAN BOOK COMPANY
New York   Cincinnati   Atlanta   Dallas   San Francisco
Copyright © 1978 by Litton Educational Publishing, Inc.

3   5   7   9   11   12   10   8   6   4   2

# ACKNOWLEDGEMENTS

Excerpt from *THE OLD MAN AND THE SEA* reprinted by permission of Charles Scribner's Sons from *THE OLD MAN AND THE SEA* by Ernest Hemingway. (copyright 1952 by Ernest Hemingway)

Excerpt from *THE SUN ALSO RISES* reprinted by permission of Charles Scribner's Sons from *THE SUN ALSO RISES* by Ernest Hemingway. (copyright 1926 by Charles Scribner's Sons)

Excerpt from "The Snows of Kilimanjaro" reprinted by permission of Charles Scribner's Sons from "The Snows of Kilimanjaro" in *THE SHORT STORIES OF ERNEST HEMINGWAY*. (copyright 1936 Ernest Hemingway)

Excerpts from "The Killers" reprinted by permission of Charles Scribner's Sons from "The Killers" from *MEN WITHOUT WOMEN* by Ernest Hemingway. (copyright 1927 Charles Scribner's Sons)

Excerpt from Carl Stephenson's *Leiningen vs. the Ants*, copyright 1938 by Carl Stephenson. Reprinted by arrangement with Ann Elmo Agency, Inc., New York

Excerpts from Mark Twain's Huckleberry Finn reprinted by permission of Harper and Row Publishers, Inc.

Excerpts from "DEADWOOD DICK," by Tom Taggart, copyright © 1953 by Samuel French, are reprinted by permission of Samuel French.

"How to Keep and Feed a Muse" by Ray Bradbury was published in *The Writer*, July 1961. Reprinted by permission of Ray Bradbury.

Excepts from *Legend of Sleepy Hollow and Other Selections*, edited by A. M. Fox, reprinted by permission of Simon and Schuster, Inc.

Excerpts from the Introduction to *Masters of the Modern Short Story*, Brief Edition, by Walter Havighurst, reprinted by permission of the publisher, Hascourt Brace Javanovich, Inc.

Excerpts from Edgar Allen Poe's "The Fall of the House of Usher" are from *Tales of the Grotesque and Arabesque*, published by Doubleday.

"The Flight of the Snowbird" by Jean Lively is reprinted by permission from *Scholastic Voice,* © 1965 by Scholastic Magazines, Inc.

"Archives," by Eugene Wildman, from The Chicago Review Anthology of Concretism, copyright © 1967, reprinted by permission of the Swallow Press.

"The Red Wheelbarrow," from *The Collected Earlier Poems of William Carlos Williams*, copyright 1938, 1951 by William Carlos Williams. Reprinted by permission of the publishers, New Directions, New York.

"Barbie Doll Goes to College," from *Pop Poems* by Ronald Gross, copyright 1967, by Ronald Gross. Reprinted by permission of the publishers, Simon & Schuster, Inc.

# TABLE OF CONTENTS

# Introduction

Creative writing involves experiencing,

*and*

1

being aware—

*then*  thinking,

*and finally,* expressing.

# Creative writing can be work.

*What a writer must try to do is to write as truly as he can. For a writer of fiction has to invent out of what he knows in order to make something not photographic, or naturalistic, or realistic, which will be something entirely new and invented out of his own knowledge.*

Ernest Hemingway

# Chapter 1

# Keeping a Record

Pictures can be fun.

Photo Album

Pictures can let you capture a fleeting moment of the past and see it again, slowly and in great detail.

Scrapbooks can do the same.

Scrapbook

Scrapbooks can keep clippings that show successes or failures, moments to remember, poems or sketches which meant something to you at some time.

And cassettes or tapes can provide still another kind of record.

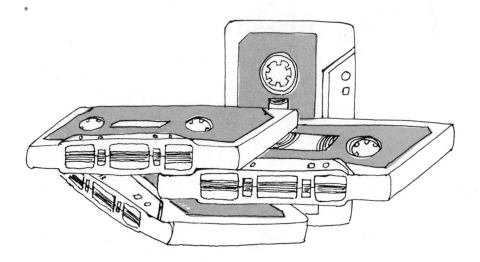

They can keep audio details which might even have gone unnoticed at the time they occurred.

## Why Keep a Record?

Most people keep some kinds of records. Records can be especially important for creative writers.

Keeping records can help you write about what you know. Of course, knowledge can be gained either from your own experiences or from the experience of others. But much of what you write about should come from what you yourself have experienced. Listen to, watch, or read about what others have done and compare it to what you know to be true. Then you can write on the basis of that comparison. But start with yourself.

## Which Record Should You Use?

Photographs, scrapbooks, and tapes are worthwhile means for recording audio or visual experience. If you have such records, keep them. However, as a writer, your primary means of recording should be writing. As MacKinlay Kantor wrote, "There is a mystery about stringing words together which cannot be solved until one has strung a lot of words together." You may never completely solve that mystery, but writing about your past and daily experiences can certainly help you investigate it more thoroughly.

You should get into the habit of scratching down impressions or ideas as they occur to you on the spur of the moment. The back of an envelope or an odd scrap of paper would probably do, but a notebook is more permanent. Perhaps you already keep a diary of some sort. Many people use one to jot down notes on the happenings of the day. For most people a diary is a very personal thing—private writings for no one else's eyes. A journal, on the other hand, might be a step in producing the writings you eventually intend to share. It doesn't matter whether you call your notebook a diary or a journal. The main thing is that you have some written record of your daily experiences, observations, and attitudes. Harriet the Spy, a well-known character in fiction, kept a journal of what happened to her each day—what she thought of her friends—or of not having any on the days she felt alone—what vegetables she didn't like and why, and what the man with the ugly growth on his face must have felt like. She kept a journal because some day she would be a writer.

Of course, different people write in different ways. Here are two pieces of student writing to help you see some of these differences in recording methods. One is from a typical private diary. The other is from the journal of a would-be writer.

### TODAY IS THE BIG DAY—OFF TO CALIFORNIA

**Got up around 6:00—left home about an hour later. Steve went with me to the bus station. I'm so glad. He kissed me good-bye a couple of times. I love him—a lot. Well, got into Chicago around noon. The trip isn't as bad as I thought it would be. Maybe it gets worse. I don't know.**

---

**The window panes are rattling, straining to keep the cold wind out and my warm summer thoughts in. I hope the glass is strong. I need my summer thoughts. They're all that's keeping me warm right now.**

**Warmth seems awfully important tonight. It's never cold at the sand dunes. Even now, in the middle of a winter night, the gulls fly, and we run in the sand, in our cutoff jeans and crazy dreams.**

Which of these two items was probably in the diary? Which was the journal entry?

Although both passages record impressions, they most likely were written for different purposes. What differences in purpose can you detect?

Which entry would probably be of greater use to its author as a source for future writing efforts?

## Things to Do

Buy something to use for a journal—a spiral bound book, a composition book, a looseleaf—whatever you think is best.

Locate some of your past records: diaries, letters, compositions, photographs, scrapbooks, or tapes. Using one or more of these sources, make your first entry in your new journal by describing one scene as you experienced it originally. If all you wrote or recorded earlier was a report of what happened, perhaps now you could add some opinions about what happened. This might be like the difference between a newsperson giving a straight report or adding commentary (his or her opinion) on what happened. If your earlier records do have commentary perhaps you have changed or might add to your point of view. Think about it, and then write.

# Chapter 2

## What to Record and How to Record It

A new journal, a new beginning. A chance to begin again, but more like a continuation of something I love. It's so clean and new now—just wait a few weeks. When I think of what this journal and I are going to go through.....

Wow! I've never kept a journal before.

I'm expressing myself now, because I know it will be important later.

*I've never kept a journal in my life, but maybe if I do, I'll learn something about myself. If I don't write every day, it's because I have something better to do than write about myself -- if that's possible!*

These initial journal entries were written by students, some obviously keeping a journal for the first time, others knowing something of what to expect. But what logically should follow such get-acquainted passages? What subjects should you put in your journal and what form should you use?

As is true in all writing, the form *(how you write)* and subject matter *(what you're writing about)* of your journal entries will be closely related. Form can vary greatly. Since it is so closely tied to what you write about, we will discuss it as we go along. This leaves us with the question of what to record, and the answer in some respects is quite simple: write about what you have experienced. In practice, however, such a challenge may seem difficult to fulfill, since often we view our lives like the child in the dialogue,

**"Where have you been?"**
**"No place."**
**"What did you do?"**
**"Nothing."**

It's true that many of us lead quite routine lives. We eat, sleep, work, watch TV, have friends, and occasionally experience the unusual. But journal entries must not be restricted to recording only unusual events. If you look back over each day, taking time to consider its events carefully, you should discover a number of happenings that may at first seem commonplace but are really worth recording. Ray Bradbury put it this way.

. . . In a lifetime, we stuff ourselves with sounds, sights, smells, tastes, and textures of people, animals, landscapes, events, large and small. We stuff ourselves with these impressions and experiences and our reaction to them . . . Into our subconscious go not only factual data but reactive data, our movement toward or away from the sensed events. These are the stuffs, the foods, on which The Muse grows. This is the storehouse, the file, to which we must return every waking hour. . . .

Receiving impressions from the world around you will, as Bradbury says, give you a storehouse of details. But simply storing these details is not enough. You must also communicate them by making entries in your journal. Only in this way—sensing details and recording details—will you later have the resources needed to create works of fiction, poetry, or drama based on your own experiences.

These two entries from student journals should help you see this need for recording in detail.

The sunset this evening was magnificent. In its beginning, the orange-colored hues spread along the horizon, making the ordinary street and trees and houses glow with the same color. And then gradually, the orange turned to red, and then to rose. The sun all the while was shrinking in size, finally manifesting itself in that one round ball of colored light about to sink behind the hills.

I finally got away for awhile. I went out west with people I didn't know very well. I've never had so much fun, besides learning a lot about myself. I always thought that it was tough for me to meet people, but after this week, I guess it really isn't. I met so many nice and friendly people up there. I can't believe it. The person who really set me straight the most was this guy named Tom. He's a Navaho Indian. This guy is unreal. I've never met a person like him. He'd sit and listen to all my problems any time I wanted to talk.

## Things to Do

Read these journal entries carefully. Which shows the greater use of detail? Take the one that uses less detail and rewrite it. Pretend you were the original writer and fill in what's missing.

Where specifically could one of them *(or both)* be improved by adding or substituting detailed description?

Could your first journal entry be improved through such addition or substitution? If in doubt, have someone look your entry over and offer suggestions.

## Record What?

These last two student entries show that writers vary in the amount of detail they record in their journals. They also show that writers vary in the kinds of entries they record. Journal entries will vary and they should, since a variety of entries gives you a wide base of recorded experiences to draw upon later.

What kinds of entries can be included in a journal? One kind can be called an incident, such as these student-written examples illustrate.

**I saw a series of heartwarming events just now. A person was having trouble getting her car out of her icy driveway. Our neighbor came to shovel our driveway for us. A boy walking along the street stopped to help the woman get out of her driveway. Our neighbor stopped shoveling to help also. Then our neighbor returned to his shoveling, and the woman gave the boy a ride to his destination.**

**A series of simple, everyday events, but how good it made me feel to see them. People caring for each other—one of the greatest things in the world.**

---

**I was looking in the rearview mirror. I guess by the time I saw the light ahead of me, it was yellow, and by then it was too late. As I entered the intersection, the light turned to that horrible red. The next lights I saw in my rearview mirror were red too. They were blinking and flashing.**

**The policeman didn't know what to make of me. The fact that I said *"Yes, sir"* and *"No, sir"* obviously stunned him. Criminals and teenagers usually don't talk like that. He gave quite a speech before he let me go.**

***"Running a red light constitutes a fine of $25.00 and on a probationary license that will be three points, and double that much for each subsequent offense,"*** **or something like that.** ***"It's obvious from your attitude that you think this whole thing is a big joke."*** **(Next he'll probably be giving me my rights.)**

"Hey. . ."
"Huh?"
"What are you doing tonight?"
"What?"
"What are you doing tonight?"
"I dunno."
"Wanna do something?"
"Like what?"
"I don't know. Like it doesn't matter. You know."
"Mmmm."
"Well?"
"Wanna go to J & J?"
"What for?"
"Something to do I guess."
"Oh, no!"
"Hey, something wrong?"
"No. You know, just something to say."
"Let's get out of here. . ."
"Yeah."
"Come on."

You have just read three journal entries. In which of the three is the time sequence of the incident most clearly stated or revealed?

What similar recording technique was used in the second and third entries?

Do your answers to these questions give you a clue as to which of the three entries might be most useful as a source for future writing? Is there an advantage to each type?

Another type of journal entry can involve a special interest—a hobby, a sport, a pastime. These next student samples are only two of any number of such entries that are possible.

**I finally got my car fixed up. I bought a new carburetor, Y pipes, cherry bomb muffler, and a new tail pipe. Everything together, along with air shocks, cost $300.00. My car could still use more work and a tune-up but I can wait until I have more time for that. Besides, I'm out of bread.**

I remember riding a horse called Bijou out on the plains. The wheat, a swaying sea of dusty gold, seemed to go on forever. The smell of earthiness, the simpleness of the fields . . . the warmth and motion . . . the wind in my hair flying golden like the grain . . . these are the things I still remember.

A horse is powerful and alive under you as you ride. The muscles beneath your legs move strongly as the lathered animal runs on and whips your face with his mane as you cling to his neck. He tosses his head in defiance of your control.

I rode away from lots of problems. The sun, the earth, and the wind always eased my mind. I long to sit on Bijou's back, aching from a long gallop and overwhelmed by the beauty around me. How I long for those summer days. Bijou and I understood each other then, because we were both fighting for our independence and a loose rein. We were both tossing our heads in defiance. What beauty there was in those long summer rides!

Can you pick out of each of these entries any specific terms or descriptions which demonstrate the author's specialized knowledge of what was being described?

Try to think of some specific ways in which such specialized knowledge could help a writer. Can specialized knowledge help a writer develop an idea for a story? Create realistic characters? Write meaningful dialogue? How?

You can describe an event or talk about a hobby. Of course, much of what you do involves other participants. Therefore, a substantial portion of your journal should include descriptions of people, especially those you meet for the first time. You may wish to use these characters in later writing.

## FABULOUS!

**What a day! I went to a picnic at the beach. It was for the kids from church. I met this guy from East High, Bob Willard. We just started talking. Then we went and played paddle ball. I got him with a water balloon. Then I got saturated by three of his. He took me home so I could change into some dry clothes. Then he asked if Rita and I wanted to go play tennis with him and this other guy.**

**What a wonderful talk we had last night, Ellen and I! It did me a world of good. Just listening to that girl speak had a soothing effect on me. It gave me encouragement to go on. Her eyes were quiet and warm and gentle. They were soft, a little like a rabbit's in a way—unlike the harsh restless eyes that pierce my world every day.**

Look back over the entries you've read so far. Notice that each one recounted or referred to a single experience lived through by its author. Sometimes the author commented on the experiences. Sometimes he or she simply related what happened.

Another type of journal entry records conclusions rather than experiences. This type of entry may be a philosophical conclusion about life in general or an introspective conclusion about yourself in particular. Be sure to include some entries of this type in your own journal. Here are some examples.

**The story of my life has the greatest author of all. The master plan was written by God and the fulfillment of that plan will make me a complete and whole person. I love life and all that goes with it! When mine is done, I will not have missed anything. What I had not done was not part of the plan for me. Those undone things would have spoiled the story, just as an alarm clock would have ruined the story of Rip Van Winkle.**

*Friday is the day before Saturday*
*And Saturday is the day before Sunday*
*And Sunday is the day before Monday.*

This thing—habit—will be my downfall yet. I think habit is a good 99% of me, and a good part of that is rotten to the core. I should be optimistic, but habit prevents the very desire.

## CRY. . . . . . . . . . . . . . . WHY????

When God said, *"Let there be light,"* what do you think he had in mind? Do you think he envisioned honky tonk Broadway or the streets of San Francisco at night? Was gaudy glitter what he planned? Or do you think he had sunsets and fireflies in mind?

I have got to be one of the most shallow persons that I know. Well shallow isn't really the word because I don't mean that in the usual way. Gullible might be better. I am so terribly susceptible to flattery. I know it's flattery. I can see right through it. But I gobble it up anyway. You know the saying *"Flattery will get you nowhere?"* In my case, that's not true.

No word is misspelled that can be read.

Walls can control people in a way, but nothing can control the mind except the mind itself.

If you were the sun, would you give the world the light it asks for, or the light it needs?

Stand in front of the tiger's cage at the zoo and look at its occupant. Be grateful that the bars separate you from the animal. Imagine how grateful the tiger must be!

Somewhere I heard that theory says you learn if you hear something repeated over and over in your sleep. I don't believe it. Everyone in school should be a genius if it were so.

It has been my observation that I, Sam Cohen, live in several worlds. I have one world that I call school, another for home, for friendship and so on. Is there really such a thing as a Sam Cohen? I don't know. At least I don't know which Sam in which world is the real Sam.

At times my world is a brilliant orange. Sometimes it is black. Sometimes it is green. Usually it is a dull gray or blue. I'd like it to be red or yellow. But it's not a painted world, so I'm not sure how to change the colors.

Notice that some of the statements are about life in general, revealing something about the author's outlook on life. The others are more about the individual authors themselves. Including both kinds of statements in a journal can assist authors in their attempts to write creatively.

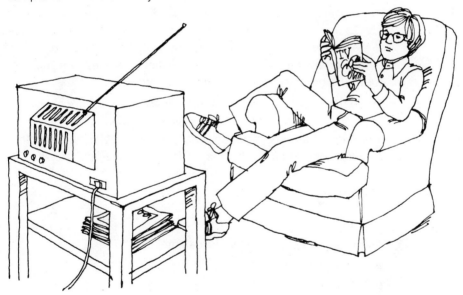

Up to this point, you've seen that writing must come from experience. Remember that experience can be gained in two ways: directly or indirectly. These second-hand, or indirect, experiences may come to us in a variety of ways. Here are some of those ways.

This evening as I was being devoured by that illustrious television program *Kung Fu* and simultaneously was attempting to read the article that was thrown together for the *TV Guide,* I began to think of the immense contrast between the philosopher Caine and the actor Carradine.

**I found this today on a poster in a little shop.**

*Desiderata*

*"Go placidly amid the noise and haste, and remember what peace there may be in silence. As far as possible without surrender be on good terms with all persons. Speak your truth quietly and clearly; and listen to others, even the dull and ignorant; they too have their story. Avoid loud and aggressive persons; they are vexations to the spirit. If you compare yourself with others, you may become vain and bitter; for always there will be greater and lesser persons than yourself. Enjoy your achievements as well as your plans.*

*Be yourself. Especially, do not feign affection. Neither be cynical about love; for in the face of all aridity and disenchantment it is perennial as the grass. Take kindly the counsel of the years, gracefully surrendering the things of youth.*

*Many fears are born of fatigue and loneliness. Beyond a wholesome discipline, be gentle with yourself. You are a child of the universe, no less than the trees and the stars; you have a right to be here. And whether or not it is clear to you, no doubt the universe is unfolding as it should.*

*Therefore be at peace with God, whatever you conceive Him to be, and whatever your labors and aspirations, in the noisy confusion of life keep peace with your soul. With all its sham, drudgery and broken dreams, it is still a beautiful world. Be careful. Strive to be happy. (Found in old Saint Paul's Church; dated 1692)"*

*Reaction to seeing the film "Hiroshima":*

*Time:* **9:45 A.M.**
*Date:* **August 8, 1945**
*Place:* **Hiroshima**

*You're a pilot flying to bomb Japan. This is not your first war mission, but you have reason to believe that this one is very different. You have a gut feeling that this is unlike any mission you've ever flown. You drop the bomb, you cover your eyes because you have been advised to do so. You open your eyes and look down. What used to be a city is nothingness. Everything is gone. Then it hits you. You've killed approximately seventy-thousand people in the time it takes to blink an eye.*

*On the table at my side was an open dictionary. A thought ran across my mind. Flash! What do all those words really mean? Can all those words control one's life? In a way they do. But aren't they just a figment of people's imaginations? Don't we just put them down to make the communication process easier? Is it always easier? Sometimes words form laws and they are books. They form stories and lots of times arguments. Sometimes they form songs and ballads and sometimes reconstruct life.*

*Words are not like chairs, carpets, doors. They don't function like people and they can't sing like frogs, yet they are used to express love, fear, hate, or anything your little heart desires.*

What different media served as sources for these entries?

What other media might you use besides these?

Notice that certain entries attempt to draw conclusions about what was read or viewed, and others do not.

Do all of the entries have the same purpose?

Remember to cite the source of a reference when quoting someone else's material in your journal.

By now you should have made at least one entry in your journal, and you also should have a fairly clear idea of the kinds of entries you can add to it as you continue to write. The choices are yours. Just remember that in order to be of use to you, your journal should include as many different types of entries as possible. Work with it every day. Imagination and persistence are the true tests of a future writer.

# Things to Do

Take a mini-field trip to a nearby location (in school or out) where you can observe a variety of vivid, detailed impressions—colors, noises, smells, textures—or a variety of people. Take a notebook or scratch paper along. Observe and record as many impressions as possible. You may want to try a shop class, a commercial kitchen, an airport or railroad station, a cemetery, a supermarket, a library, a factory, a discount store, or a pet shop. Choose a convenient place that offers a variety of impressions.

Upon returning from your field trip, look over your notes. Write a detailed journal entry from the impressions you recorded.

Try as many mini-trips as possible. Keep on with your journal entries.

Write up your experience from one field trip in at least two different forms. Review the different examples in this chapter to give yourself an idea of the possible types.

# Chapter 3

## Words

Artists and writers have much in common. Although the artist uses color and form and the writer uses language, both try to portray life as they see it. The artist produces lines and shapes: the writer produces words and sentences. In the end, each produces a finished product, a creative work, born of experience and imagination.

Look again at the two works of art here. You don't have to study them long to notice the different techniques used by the artists. Yet each artist had the same tools available. Each artist had to make a series of choices as to which techniques to employ. Different writers have the same tools—words—available to them. Which words they use, and how they put them together is a matter of the writer's choice. Now, as you work with words, you should study works and techniques of as many different authors as you can. Experiment with different techniques in your journal. You will find gradually that your own unique style of writing will evolve. You'll always continue to experiment, but the techniques you have to think about now will become habits as you continue to work with words.

# Creating Imagery

What words should you choose to include in your writing? What techniques of word choice should a creative writer know?

In a way, the difference between these two pictures defines your job as a writer using words. Writers are expected to fill in the details for readers, but with words, not lines or colors. The words you choose should create a mental picture or image within the reader's mind, by appealing to the five senses of sight, touch, hearing, taste, and smell. The use of this kind of sensory detail is called imagery. Imagery serves as a basis for the communicating of experience. Ray Bradbury stresses its importance by asking,

**Why all this insistence on the senses? Because in order to convince your reader that he is *there*, you must assault each of his senses, in turn, with color, sound, taste, and texture. If your reader feels the sun on his flesh, the wind fluttering his shirt sleeves, half your fight is won. The most improbable tales can be made believable, if your reader, through his senses, feels certain that he stands at the middle of events. He cannot refuse, then, to participate. The logic of events always gives way to the logic of the senses.**

Bradbury is telling us what every creative writer must never forget: don't tell your readers—show them. To stress this point, Bradbury doesn't even use the term *show*. He uses a stronger word than that. He says you must *"assault"* the senses of your reader.

Here are two selections. The first is from a student journal; the other is from Mark Twain's *The Adventures of Huckleberry Finn*. Notice how the two writers use details.

**The flight was great. It was a trip. I loved it. I just loved looking out of the window. I'm flying all the time. We had dinner on it. It was good. It's so nice. It only cost $131.26 on the "See America" fare.**

**All the stores was along one street. They had white domestic awnings in front, and the country-people hitched their horses to the awning-posts. There was empty dry-goods boxes under the awnings, and loafers roosting on them all day long, whittling them with their Barlow knives; and chawing tobacco, and gaping and yawning and stretching—a mighty ornery lot. They generly had on yellow straw hats most as wide as an umbrella, but didn't wear no coats nor waistcoats; they called one another Bill,**

and Buck, and Hank, and Joe, and Andy, and talked lazy and drawly, and used considerable many cuss-words. There was as many as one loafer leaning up against every awning-post, and he most always had his hands in his britches pockets, except when he fetched them out to lend a chaw of tobacco or scratch.

Which passages within each quotation are general statements giving an overall impression? Note the specific details or imagery within each quotation used to back up the more generalized statements. Now look at the two quotations again. Which quotation achieves a better balance between the general and the specific?

What would have happened to the balance achieved in the second quotation if the author had described everything, every detail, in this scene without having been selective?

In the first quotation, the repeated use of a pronoun contributes to the lack of detail. Which pronoun is it?

The casual expressions used in the first quotation don't really provide the specific imagery needed. Note how this compares to the use of dialect in the second quotation.

Whether the author of a work is Mark Twain or you, words are essentially what the writer has to work with. Make words work for you. Select those words which will create exactly the images you wish to portray—nothing more, nothing less.

## Things to Do

Here are some generalizations. For each one, you will have to supply sufficient sensory detail to support the statement given.

    a. I closed my eyes in order to be aware of the variety of textures in my hands.
    b. She had a fascinating face.
    c. Each mouthful presented a strange variety of tastes.
    d. The room had a cluttered appearance.
    e. I'd never heard a sound like that before.
    f. He walked in an unusual manner.
    g. A mixture of odors filled the room.
    h. Suddenly everything was peaceful.

Go back to the journal entry you wrote as a result of the mini-field trip. Read it again and see if you achieved a balance between the general and the specific. Did you provide a sufficient amount of sensory detail? If necessary, rewrite the entry now.

## Using Figurative Language

Vivid descriptions can be accomplished by providing readers with specific imagery, but writers frequently use another technique of wording that you should not overlook—making comparisons. Using comparisons allows a writer to go beyond a single description by giving an alternative, complimentary, or contrasting view. In this respect, a comparison can often clarify a description.

> *"How large is it?"*
> *"Big."*
> *"Whata ya mean, 'big'?"*
> *"Bigger than a breadbox."*
> *"Oh."*

Clarification is one reason a writer uses comparison. Some comparisons not only are informative but can demonstrate your creativity as well. This dual purpose is most often found in the use of figurative comparisons or figures of speech. Figures of speech are condensed comparisons which relate two unlike things having one or more common characteristics. A figure of speech can provide the reader with a vivid sensory description and give a pleasant surprise at the same time.

Here are two pictures that illustrate a figure of speech. They compare two unlike things which have a common characteristic.

Try expressing this pictorial figure of speech in as many ways as you can.

Since figures of speech compare two unlike things, they consist of two parts. Together they form a figure of speech describing a common quality, in this case whiteness.

As you probably realized when you put the two pictures into words, figures of speech can be constructed in a variety of ways. How you construct a figure of speech, that is, the specific words you choose, will determine the kind of figure it is. For example, if you stated the visual comparison by saying, "The paper is snow white," your choice of words would have created a *metaphor*. If you said, "The paper is as white as snow," or, "The paper is like snow," you'd be using a figure of speech called a *simile*. Metaphor is an implied comparison. Simile is a direct comparison using the terms *like* or *as*.

A third figure of speech is called *personification,* giving human qualities, or the qualities of a *person* to something inanimate. If you tried to describe how you felt looking at your blank journal with nothing to say you might end up writing "The blank paper stared at me," or "I felt the paper's eyes on me." By giving the paper human qualities you have used personification.

Besides allowing you to demonstrate your creativity in a concise manner, figures of speech relate to another important aspect of your writing. Figures of speech are another way of showing your readers instead of telling them. By suggesting a tie between two items not usually related, you allow your readers to make their own associations, to use their own imaginations by seeing the re- lationship for themselves. And at times, these relationships can be very powerful and dramatic.

Like any technique in writing, however, figures of speech should not be used to the exclusion of all other methods of achieving viv- idness. Notice how Twain employs metaphor, simile, and per- sonification in this passage.

**It was one of these regular summer storms. It would get so dark that it looked all blue-black outside, and lovely; and the rain would thrash along by so thick that the trees off a little ways looked dim and spider-webby; and here would come a blast of wind that would bend the trees down and turn up the pale underside of the leaves; and then a perfect ripper of a gust would follow along and set the branches to tossing their arms as if they was just wild; and next, when**

it was just about the bluest and blackest—*fst!* it was as bright as glory, and you'd have a little glimpse of treetops a-plunging about away off yonder in the storm, hundreds of yards further than you could see before; dark as sin again in a second, and now you'd hear the thunder let go with an awful crash, and then go rumbling, grumbling, tumbling, down the sky towards the under side of the world, like rolling empty barrels down-stairs—where it's long stairs and they bounce a good deal, you know.

Try to identify the figures of speech used by Twain. In relation to the total length of the passage and the intensity of the action being described, do you think he overused figurative language? Why or why not?

What effect can a writer achieve by limiting the use of figurative language?

The subjects shown here can easily be identified. Each has a distinct quality that's so well known that it's easy for most people to recognize what that quality is. This associative quality can be used by writers to create another figure of speech. This figure of speech is called *allusion*.

An allusion describes a person, place, or event by figuratively comparing it to another person, place, or event whose qualities are so well known that no explanation is needed. What quality does each of the above illustrations depict? Who would be a better benefactor—Santa Claus or Scrooge? Do you know of a place you might think of as a Garden of Eden? Have you ever referred to something as a Mickey Mouse situation? Can you describe a situation as Sisyphean or a Last Stand? Why might you compare something to Noah and his Ark?

Allusions are useful as concise comparisons, but they have to be employed with care. Like other figures of speech, they should not be used too often. Though they must be immediately recognizable, they must not be so inevitable that the reader anticipates them. An effective allusion, although readily identified, comes as a surprise to the reader. Use allusions to create well-known but unexpected associations.

# Things to Do

Practice working with the figures of speech you have just read about. Try writing a simile for a tired person, something cold, something ugly, something fragile. Write a metaphor for someone angry, shy, brave, hungry. Personify a chair, a hose, a storm, the sun, a fence. Identify four or five persons, events, or places with strong enough identifiable quality to use in allusion.

## Fatigued Figures and Mixed Metaphors

As you write, try to avoid phrases that are too commonly used. If one of the purposes in using a figure of speech is to allow readers to use their imaginations in making associations, then you as a writer should make your comparisons as creative as possible. This means avoiding clichés, those worn-out tired associations that long ago went out of style. Here are some common clichés, with some pieces missing. See if you can mentally fill in the blanks.

**The baby is pretty as a _____ .**
**The man looked as old as the _____ .**
**The puppy's hair is smooth as _____ . .**
**The doughnut was as hard as a _____ .**
**My friend was as strong as _____ . .**
**Filling in these blanks is easy as _____ .**

But ease in making such comparisons should be a danger signal to a writer.

These overused associations have their place, but not in creative description. In using figures of speech, you, as an author, must decide whether or not you want your reader to use imagination, not memory. You will employ figures of speech, but like any good thing too much of it may make your writing bite the dust. Here, for instance, is a description of Santiago, the old man in Hemingway's *The Old Man and the Sea,* in which Hemingway includes some figures of speech but resorts more to the use of specific details, which was discussed earlier.

**The old man was thin and gaunt with deep wrinkles in the back of his neck. The brown blotches of the benevolent skin cancer the sun brings from its reflection on the tropic sea were on his cheeks. The blotches ran well down the sides of his face, and his hands had the deep-creased scars from handling heavy fish on the cords. But none of these scars were fresh. They were as old as erosions in a fishless desert.**

How much of this excerpt is made up of specific detail?

How does the use of only one simile and its placement contribute to the effectiveness of the description?

How does the nature of the simile, that is, Hemingway's choice of comparison, contribute to the description of a fisherman?

What quality would have been lost in the description had Hemingway used a cliché such as "old as the hills" to describe Santiago? Can you think up a fresh way to describe old?

Some figures of speech involve only one association. Other figurative comparisons, however, can suggest a number of associations. Snow, for example, when compared to paper has only one associative quality, whiteness. But to say that, "Life is a road," conjures up numerous associations—it's bumpy, it twists, it forks, it's continuous—all of which you might want to connote in describing life.

But just as lack of freshness creates the hazards of cliché, producing extended metaphors has additional pitfalls for unwary writers. In developing a sustained figure of speech, be careful not to mix your metaphors. Compare the use of extended metaphor in these two passages.

As I walked home, the storm began. First the wind struck me with the force of a prizefighter's fist. Its claws snatched at my clothes as I bent forward resisting its explosive burst of force. Suddenly I could not breathe. I turned my head gasping as it snatched the air from my lungs like a giant vacuum pump. Finally, I succeeded in reaching the house by walking backwards, all the while feeling the wind thump on my back like a thousand horses straining for the finish line.

It was very pleasant, when I stayed late in town, to launch myself into the night, especially if it was dark and tempestuous, and set sail from some bright village parlor or lecture room, with a bag of rye or Indian meal upon my shoulder, for my snug harbor in the woods, having made all tight without and withdrawn under hatches with a merry crew of thoughts, leaving only my outer man at the helm, or even tying up the helm when it was plain sailing. I had many a genial thought by the cabin fire "as I sailed." I was never cast away nor distressed in any weather, though I encountered some severe storms.

from Thoreau's Walden

What initial metaphor does the first passage establish? What else does the author use to describe wind?

What basic metaphor is established in the second passage?

What does the author play upon to sustain his description of leaving town?

What successive and climactic advantages does the sustained metaphor in the second passage create that are not achieved in the first passage?

Try experimenting with extended metaphors in your journal, but remember that once you establish a figurative association, you must develop it consistently. Don't confuse your reader.

**_Use the right word, not its second cousin._**

Mark Twain

# Using Opposites

*Setting:* a rainy day. The hero walks into the house wringing wet and announces in dry tones, *"What a beautiful day!"*

This scene illustrates another figure of speech, *irony*. Here, instead of using a metaphor such as, *"It's raining buckets,"* or a personification, *"The sky is crying,"* the speaker described the scene by referring to something which was the exact opposite, *"a beautiful day."* This type of figure of speech is called irony. It states the opposite of what exists, in a context where the real situation is implied through the contradiction.

Though the method is always the same, a writer's or speaker's purpose for using irony can vary. Our rained-out hero used it to express disappointment. Other users may express disapproval, *"I like your new outfit,"* or even bitterness, *"What the world needs is a little more hate."* Other types of irony use different methods to accomplish different purposes.

A statement that contains its own contradiction or surface absurdity, thereby making its meaning uncertain, is called a *paradox*. *"We destroyed the town in order to save it."* How can you save it by destroying it? *"We must arm ourselves for peace."* Bearing arms seems to contradict the notion of peace.

You can compare an object to something different but show similar qualities. You can give life to something that has none. You can use words to create opposite effects or contradictions.

Metaphor, simile, personification, allusion, irony, and paradox—these are some of the figures of speech you can use to create vivid impressions in your writing. There are others, but these are the ones you'll probably use most often, and any handbook of literature can acquaint you with additional types.

Practice using the different figures as you write in your journal. Use them appropriately and sparingly—like salt.

## Things to Do

Each of the following figures of speech is a cliché describing a common condition. Choose at least one and write a paragraph using sufficient sensory detail to create the same overall impression without stating the cliché. Remember a cliché is an overused expression, and that's why we're not using it anymore.

**She was as pretty as a picture.**
**Her hair was as smooth as silk.**
**My doughnut was as hard as nails.**
**The child was quiet as a mouse.**
**She swims like a rock.**
**He was as strong as Hercules.**
**He had the patience of Job.**

Each of the following figures can be logically extended. Choose at least one and write a short paragraph which consistently develops the stated comparison.

**a scout leader as a sheep dog**
**a sporting event as a battle**
**a book as a friend**
**a storm as a bully**
**a setting sun as an artist**

The following quotations could be taken as either literal or ironic statements. Assuming that they are meant to be taken ironically, choose one and write a paragraph which establishes a setting and a character. Then describe the scene so that the quoted statement serves as a final, logical, but ironic sentence spoken by the character you've created.

**"Yeah, I know. It was owned by a little old lady who only drove it to church on Sunday."**

**"Sure I'd like to go out with you. Anytime."**

"Now that's the kind of book I'd like to keep under my pillow every night."

"Why it's just what I always wanted."

Choose one of the following paradoxical statements (a statement containing a contradiction) and write a brief explanation of it as an adult character in a story explaining the statement to a younger person.

"Our country must arm for peace."

"Your left hand must not know what your right hand is doing."

"He helps himself who helps others."

"For whoever would save his life will lose it, whoever loses his life for my sake will find it."

## Choosing the Right Word

What does a flower do to your nose? What do rotten eggs do? Fresh bread? Old clothes? Which words best describe each of these sensations? Is there a "right" or most appropriate word to use for the meaning you wish to convey?

Writers of English have the advantage of using a language that is very rich in synonyms, both from native stock and from words borrowed from almost every language known. But this advantage can pose a problem in word choice. At times there seem to be almost too many synonyms. Here are some points that should help you pick the right word at the right time.

Your first consideration should be the denotative-connotative qualities of the words you select. Denotation is the explicit or dictionary meaning of a word. Connotation refers to its suggestive, personal, or emotive meaning. Of course, words cannot be precisely labeled as possessing one distinct quality or the other.

Look at the following quoted sentence. As you read it, see first how many words you could place in the blank that would have the correct denotation (dictionary meaning). Then from that variety, choose those that you think would have the most appropriate connotations (suggested meaning).

**The _____ of old roses permeated the room.**

Why would the term *blend* not be correct for this sentence?

How would the term *effluvium* create a contrast to most of the other descriptive terms used in this sentence?

Why would the connotations of words like *stink, reek,* or *stench* probably be inappropriate to this sentence?

How about the terms *aroma* or *fragrance?* Would they be inappropriate? There are a lot of words to choose from. Make sure the one you choose has the right connotation.

What additional information about the characters or setting would be helpful in choosing a term with the "right" connotation for this sentence?

As you use words, make as many knowing choices as possible. Don't be afraid to change a word that may give the reader the wrong impression. And, when in doubt, use your thesaurus and dictionary.

Flower terms present one set of connotative problems; other subjects—humans, for example—involve additional choices.

Imagine this scene:

*Nurse:*     "Doctor, your patient is waiting to be examined in the next room."

*Doctor:*     "Yes, I'll see him as soon as he's naked."

Many terms, especially those dealing with human conditions, require that we make our connotative choices with extra care. The choice made in determining the appropriate term to describe the old roses was primarily a matter of matching the right word to the total context of the sentence. In the doctor-nurse example, it is the social implications of the terms that are of primary importance. The term *naked* has socially unacceptable connotations that the term *disrobed* avoids. To employ a more acceptable word to describe harsh reality is to use a *euphemism*. This kind of verbal anesthetic is often used to describe such conditions as old age, poverty, stupidity, death, argument, or almost any condition about which people might be sensitive. Since many people fear the thought of dying, they cope with it by saying when I "pass away." Somehow that seems to soften the idea of death a bit.

Should you use euphemisms in your writing? Certainly you must be sensitive to their application. But there are times when you will consciously *not* want to use them, if for some reason you wish to achieve the stark effect which comes from avoiding a soft touch. The title of Norman Mailer's work, *The Naked and the Dead* shows this effect very clearly. He could hardly have achieved the same impact with a title like *The Disrobed and the Departed*.

So here you are again with a choice on your hands. Make that choice. *You're* the author now. Know what words can do. Know what you want to say and make the words work for you. Use a dictionary or a thesaurus. If words are your tools, these books are your tool box.

Word selection is neither easy nor simple. It requires care and a knowledge of the language. But words are the basic elements of your writing. With their precise use, you can produce vivid imagery, figurative associations, and endless subtlety of meaning. And these are the beginnings of your art.

## Things to Do

Choose one of the following lists of words and write a sentence using each word. Vary your sentences so that they reflect the difference in meaning for each word.

| | | |
|---|---|---|
| thin | loud | soft |
| skinny | blaring | tender |
| slight | noisy | flocculent |
| slim | raucous | sensitive |
| slender | discordant | lissome |
| emaciated | cacophonous | flabby |
| bony | deafening | mellow |
| attenuated | shrill | soggy |
| lean | clamorous | supple |
| scrawny | piercing | smooth |

The following statements describe various acts or conditions. For each expression write as many different euphemisms as you can, putting each in sentence form. Remember a euphemism tries to make the word less harsh, not so hard to take.

> **to be fired from a job**
> **to steal**
> **to kill**
> **to torture**
> **to argue**
> **to be poor**

Rewrite the following passage by replacing the underlined terms with other words.

> The *child sat* on the *short stool twisting* his *hat* in his *hands,* while *thinking* that he would never see his *mother again.*

Now that you've replaced all of the underlined words with other words, see if it would have been better to leave some and change just a few. There are many different ways to do it. When you've settled on the final paragraph, compare yours to that of someone else in your class. Discuss your different choices and see if you can learn why what you did was good, or how it could still be improved.

*That's a very good way to learn the craft of writing—from reading.*

William Faulkner

*A story is not the same thing when it ends as it was when it began.*

Eudora Welty

*Just get into the habit of putting words down, and try not to miss a day.*

Emily Hahn

# Chapter 4

## Sentences

You've probably heard the saying, *"The whole is greater than the sum of its parts."* This holds true for many things including creative writing. Words are the basic units of meaning in writing, and as you've seen, their meanings can be conveyed in a variety of ways. But one word out of context or a thousand words in isolation cannot convey meaning the way words carefully put together into sentences can.

### Sentence Structures

The most obvious characteristic of sentence structure is length. Some sentences *(like this one)* are long, containing complex associations of interrelated structures which connect ideas through the use of various grammatical patterns. Some are short. And others strike a balance between the two extremes. Your problem is to try to figure out when and where to use which. Right?

Read the following passage from Ernest Hemingway's book, *The Sun Also Rises.*

> **The bus climbed steadily up the road. The country was barren and rocks stuck up through the clay. There was no grass beside the road. Looking back we could see the country spread out below. Far back the fields were squares of green and brown on the hillsides. Making the horizon were the brown mountains. They were strangely shaped.**

What effect is achieved by the shortness of Hemingway's sentences?

The following quotation from Carl Stephenson's story, *Leiningen versus the Ants,* is like the Hemingway passage in that it uses short sentences, but it differs from the Hemingway quotation in several significant ways. Stephenson's passage describes the climax or high point of an adventure story. A man is literally running for his life through a field of man-eating ants, which by this point have completely covered his body.

> **Frantic with pain, he almost plunged into the river. To be ripped and slashed to shreds by piranhas? Already he was running the return journey, knocking ants from his gloves and jacket, brushing them from his bloodied face, squashing them to death under his clothes.**
>
> **A stone in the path ... too weak to avoid it ... the planter stumbled and collapsed. He tried to rise ... he must be pinned under a rock ... it was impossible ... the slightest movement was impossible ...**
>
> **Then all at once he saw, starkly clear and huge, and, right before his eyes, furred with ants, towering and swaying in its death agony, the pampas stag. In six minutes—gnawed to the bones. God, he *couldn't* die like that! And something outside him seemed to drag him to his feet. He tottered. He began to stagger forward again.**

Why is Stephenson's use of short sentences especially appropriate to what he is describing?

How do the Hemingway and Stephenson passages differ in terms of what is being described in each?

Though Stephenson's sentences are not all short, he continually achieves the impression of brevity through a variety of structuring techniques. Note the different punctuation marks he uses to isolate details or pieces of action.

In the first paragraph he uses two techniques. What verb form is repeatedly used in the last sentence of the paragraph to move the description at a rapid pace? What structure is used in the second sentence to accomplish this same effect?

Stephenson uses a variety of techniques to isolate detail rather than repeat one technique throughout.

Now let's look at the possible effect of long sentences. What they can achieve is illustrated in the following quotation from Hemingway's "The Snows of Kilimanjaro." Here Hemingway describes what happens to Harry, as seen by Harry after his death. He is being flown by a pilot-friend named Compie to the top of Mount Kilimanjaro. Earlier, Hemingway has told us that the top of the mountain is called "the House of God." If possible, read the quotation aloud, or have someone read it to you as you follow along.

**And then instead of going on to Arusha they turned left, he [*Compie*] evidently figured that they had the gas, and looking down he [*Harry*] saw a pink sifting cloud, moving over the ground, and in the air, like the first snow in a blizzard, that comes from nowhere, and he knew the locusts were coming up from the South. Then they began to climb and they were going to the East it seemed, and then it darkened and they were in a storm, the rain so thick it seemed like flying through a waterfall, and then they were out and Compie turned his head and grinned and pointed and there, ahead, all he could see, as wide as all the world, great, high, and unbelievably white in the sun, was the square top of Kilimanjaro. And then he knew that there was where he was going.**

Of the three sentences in this passage, which two are longest?

Where are these two sentences placed within the paragraph?

What purposes does the repeated use of the term *then* serve within the passage?

In contrast to the effect Stephenson achieved in his use of short sentences to isolate detail, what effect does Hemingway achieve through his use of long sentences? Note how the placement of the two long sentences contributes to this effect.

In utilizing long sentences, writers must choose carefully the words they use to connect the interrelated elements of their descriptions. Normally, they will have to use a variety of different connecting words and phrases in order to indicate both progression and the relationship of ideas. Hemingway, however, breaks this norm and achieves a special effect. What connector does he use in an unusually repetitious manner?

Now look at the following quotation of the first four verses from the book of Genesis.

**In the beginning God created the heaven and the earth.**

**And the earth was without form, and void; and darkness was upon the face of the deep. And the Spirit of God moved upon the face of the waters.**

**And God said, Let there be light: and there was light.**

**And God saw the light, that it was good; and God divided the light from the darkness.**

Compare the effects of the repeated connector used in Genesis and that used by Hemingway.

Try to vary your sentence length—long, short, or in between. Short sentences or isolated phrases have a definite effect in writing. Decide what effect you want. If you don't like it, change it.

Although sentence length is the most obvious feature of sentence structure, it is not the only one. Sentences can also be categorized as *loose* or *periodic*. A loose sentence makes an initial major statement with an independent clause and then may add to that statement with dependent clauses or modifying phrases. A periodic sentence is structured in the reverse manner. It begins with dependent clauses or modifying elements and then concludes with an independent or main clause.

This passage is taken from the opening of Daniel Defoe's classic *Robinson Crusoe*. Notice the sentence structure.

**I was born, in the year 1632, in the city of York, of a good family, though not of that country, my father being a foreigner of Bremen, who settled first at Hull. He got a good estate by merchandise, and, leaving off his trade, lived afterwards at York, from whence he had married my mother, whose relations were named Robinson, a very good family in that country, and from whom I was called Robinson Kreutznaer; but, by the usual corruption of words in England, we are now called—nay, we call ourselves, and write our name—Crusoe; and so my companions always called me.**

Can you identify the independent clause that opens each of Defoe's two sentences?

What effect does Defoe achieve by placing each independent clause first, as opposed to inserting it later on in the sentence? Now look at this rewrite of the Defoe passage.

**I was born in 1632, in the city of York. I came from a good family though not of that country. My father was a foreigner of Bremen. He settled first at Hull. He got a good estate by merchandise, and, leaving off his trade, lived afterwards at York, from whence he had married my mother, whose relations were named Robinson, and from whom I was called Robinson Kreutznaer; but, by the usual corruption of words in England, we are now called—nay, we call ourselves, and write our name—Crusoe; and so my companions always called me.**

Count the loose sentences in this rewritten passage.

This excessive use of loose sentences creates two problems. One problem is a series of repetitive, identical sentence structures. This repetition does not create meaningful emphasis and serves no purpose. Notice how it detracts from the readability of the passage.

Look at the last sentence of the rewrite and you will find the second problem. When you read the original version, perhaps you thought the sentences long but not excessively so. Now, in the second version the last sentence does seem too long. What was changed to create this impression of excessive length? Not only is the sentence long, but it has too many qualifying elements tacked on to one independent clause, with no apparent end or climax. This problem is especially noticeable because there are a number of short sentences just preceding the long one.

*I got into my bones the essential structure of the normal British sentence—which is a noble thing.*

Sir Winston Churchill

In contrast to loose sentences, periodic sentences are less common, accomplish different effects, and have their own hazards. Read this excerpt from Da Vinci's *Notebooks* very carefully.

**If the painter wishes to see enchanting beauties, he has the power to produce them. If he wishes to see monstrosities, whether terrifying, or ludicrous and laughable, or pitiful, he has the power and authority to create them. If he wishes to produce towns or deserts, if in the hot season he wants cool and shady places, or in the cold season warm places, he can make them. If he wants valleys, if from high mountaintops he wants to survey vast stretches of country, if beyond he wants to see the horizon on the sea, he has the power to create all this; and likewise, if from deep valleys he wants to see high mountains or from high mountains deep valleys and beaches. Indeed, whatever exists in the universe, whether in essence, in act, or in the imagination, the painter has first in his mind and then in his hands. His hands are of such excellence that they can present to our view simultaneously whatever well-proportioned harmonies real things exhibit piecemeal.**

Locate the sentences which are constructed periodically in this passage.

Loose sentences tend to emphasize the thought being expressed in the independent clause by placing it first. Can you see what effects involving anticipation can be achieved in periodic sentences by placing the main clause last?

All the sentences in this passage are periodic except the last. What purpose does this single, final, loose sentence serve?

Imagine that Da Vinci had not provided the final loose sentence for this passage. What negative effects for the reader might be created in a piece of writing, if all the sentences were structured periodically?

Long or short, loose or periodic. These are four structural variations you will be using in your writing. You may not always be aware of them as you put your thoughts on paper, but keep them in mind as you look your work over. If you notice that certain passages don't sound smooth or build as they should, check to see if you have used these four types of sentence structures to their best advantages. Balance your writing and use the strengths of each structure.

Label each of these pictures. Then put the first sequence into a sentence. Then the second.

For the first set of pictures you probably came up with something like, "The baseball player threw the ball." For the second, "The baseball was thrown by the baseball player." Do you notice the differences in their constructions? The first construction is called *active voice*. The doer in the sentence is the subject, and the single verb is stated in past tense form. The second sentence is called *passive voice*. Here the object receiving the action serves as the subject, and the verb is made up of a past participle plus a form of *to be*.

Generally, most writers use the active voice much more frequently than the passive. The active voice is just that—active. It creates sentences which are more forceful than the weaker passive voice can create.

But don't slight the passive voice entirely. It can be useful, even though it tends not to be emphatic. For example, you might find yourself writing some sentences like these.

**The Smith's summer house was being redecorated.**
**Halters were not being worn in the city that season.**
**Rain had been forecast for the next day.**

The doers in these sentences are not named. Who are they? Is it important to know exactly? Probably not.

Or, you might use the passive voice in this manner.

**The white house was demolished by bulldozers.**
**The woman was attacked by unknown assailants.**

Who are the doers in these sentences? Note in each case, that the receiver of the action is being emphasized by being placed first.

Or, when used in dialogue, the passive voice can sometimes suggest a character's motive.

**"The theft is being thoroughly investigated."**
**"The gift was sent by me."**

In the first example perhaps the speaker does not wish to state who is investigating the theft. In the second sentence, why might the speaker be avoiding the use of the word *I* as the subject of the sentence?

These examples show that passive voice has its place. Most of your writing, however, should use the active voice. Check your sentence structure to see that your ideas are forcefully stated. If you do use the passive voice, do it for a specific purpose. Don't weaken your writing by drifting into the passive through lack of control.

## Equal is Equal, Except. . .

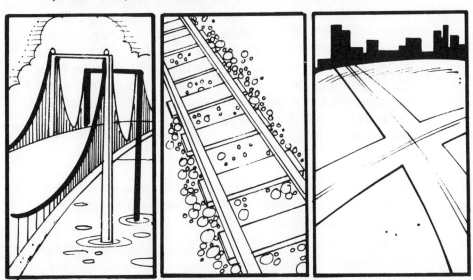

Use these illustrations to test your visual perception. What do the three pictures have in common?

Did you recognize that each picture contains two or more like elements? The first repeats similar objects; the second balances two objects; and the third contrasts two objects.

This use of like elements is called *parallelism*. Visually, artists and photographers use parallel objects and lines to create dramatic forces of emphasis. Verbally, writers too can use parallel constructions—words, phrases, clauses, or sentences—to achieve emphasis and clarity. Read this passage written by Sir Winston Churchill, one of the most dynamic writers of our century. He wrote this speech as an address to the people of England, during the darkest days of World War II. If possible, listen to a recording or tape of the original speech, as you read it here.

**The British Empire and the French Republic, linked together in their cause and their need, will defend to the death their native soil, aiding each other like good comrades to the utmost of their strength. Even though large tracts of Europe and many old and famous States have fallen or may fall into the grip of the Gestapo and all the odious apparatus of Nazi rule, we shall not flag or fail. We shall go on to the end. We shall fight in France, we shall fight on the seas and oceans, we shall fight with growing confidence and growing strength in the air, we shall defend our island, whatever the cost may be. We shall fight on the beaches, we shall fight on the landing grounds, we shall fight in the fields and in the streets, we shall fight in the hills, we shall never surrender, and even if, which I do not for a moment believe, this island or a large part of it were subjugated and starving, then our Empire beyond the seas, armed and guarded by the British Fleet, would carry on the struggle, until, in God's good time, the New World, with all its power and might, steps forth to the rescue and the liberation of the old.**

What specific construction does Churchill use to create parallelism both between and within all of the sentences in the center portion of the quotation?

In creating these parallel structures, did he use loose constructions or periodic? To what advantage?

Besides the use of parallel clauses, can you locate some of the many paired words and phrases he uses throughout the passage?

Note the effect created by this pairing of minor elements. Compare it to the major repetitive kind of parallelism provided by the clauses. Under different circumstances, Churchill's use of parallelism might be considered excessive and extreme. How can his extensive use of this technique be justified in this passage?

Parallelism, then, can be created either by pairing or repeating like structures. Closely associated with this technique is a similar use of pairing or repeating structures which contain elements that are not totally alike.

Look at these statements.

**He was attired in a splendid morning coat, a silk cravat, striped trousers, polished shoes, and dirty socks.**

**The job of every sheep dog is to herd the sheep, to protect the flock, and to eat a lamb for supper.**

Each of these statements has a surprise. Each pulls you up short by presenting dissimilar or perpendicular ideas within similar or parallel constructions.

This technique is called anticlimax. With parallel structures, we usually expect the presentation of like rather than unlike concepts. Repeated structures normally build to a semantic as well as a structural climax. Both of these points were illustrated by the Churchill passage. Since readers expect meaning and structure to go hand in hand, they are surprised by a break in this continuity. Don't overdo this use of surprise. Save it for special occasions.

Moderation and appropriateness are key things to keep in mind when using parallel constructions. Since parallelism is such a powerful and dramatic technique of writing, it should be employed with discretion. Minor forms of it can be used often for clarity and economy. Major forms like the repeated use of clauses or whole sentences should be saved for your most forceful passages. At all times be sure that your constructions are grammatically accurate. Elements which you intend to be parallel but mistakenly construct so they are not, may confuse your reader.

## Things to Do

The following paragraph is made up entirely of short sentences. Read the paragraph carefully. Decide which statements need to be emphasized. Then rewrite the paragraph, retaining the short sentences where you need them to emphasize detail or advance the action, while combining other statements to form longer sentences to provide variety. As you create these new constructions, try to achieve a balance between loose sentences, which can create initial emphasis, and periodic sentences, which tend to make the reader anticipate a major statement.

**Toby saw the wallet fall. It fell out of the woman's handbag. She had just been getting out of her car. It was a dark-blue Mark IV. She closed the car door. She turned. Her skirt swirled. It created a flash of silken colors. Just then she slung her shoulder-bag around. Her shoulder was deeply tanned. The wallet felt. At the same time, she slammed the car door. The slam was soft. It sounded like a refrigerator closing. She did not notice the wallet strike the ground. Toby stood there. He watched her walk away. She strolled casually toward the shopping center. Her skirt swung rhythmically. She was oblivious to what had heppened. He waited. Finally she disappeared into Marcelle's Boutique. Toby walked slowly to the wallet. He was cautious. He peered at it. It was light blue. It cast a delicate sheen in the hot sun. Toby gently flipped it open with his foot. The wallet bulged. It wouldn't open all the way. The tips of a great many green bills were sticking out of the top. He placed his foot over the wallet. He stood there. He looked up. He stared across the length of the parking lot. Suddenly, the sunlight flashed on the glass doors of Marcelle's Boutique.**

Here's a passage that is written mainly in the passive voice. Rewrite the paragraph, substituting the active voice wherever needed. Retain the passive where you consider it appropriate.

**The scene was Wimbledon, England. The stands were filled by quiet, intense spectators, long before the opening matches were scheduled to begin. Their politeness was obvious as the final match of the day was waited for by the crowd. Finally the time arrived, and Jackie Conrad, the American finalist, was stared at by everyone as she entered. A steady, business-like manner was assumed by Jackie as the opening serve was delivered by her. An overhead was blasted by her and a puff of dust was kicked up on the back line. "Out," yelled the linesman. A frozen smile was placed on her face by Jackie. The game was returned to by her. A long, dissappointing afternoon was to be endured by those who had paid to see her perform.**

Each of the following sentences was written with deliberate non-parallel structure. Rewrite each one. Create word, phrase, clause, or sentence parallelism in order to clarify the meaning or achieve appropriate emphasis.

**He thought of all bankers as being greedy, malicious, and not to be trusted.**

**Her diet was based upon a program of taking hikes, counting calories, and not eating any snacks.**

**The singer neither understood his own score nor the conductor's directions.**

**Not only was Edith tired but quite frantic as well.**

**He tore through the room. While doing so, he smashed the furniture. He also waved his arms. Finally, he screamed that no one understands him.**

**Leaving home was her only desire. To leave her place of residence would solve everything. But the departure would not be easy.**

Choose one of the above statements. Rewrite it again to form an anticlimax by adding or substituting a discordant or surprise idea at the end.

Go to your journal and read carefully one or more of your most recent entries. Pay particular attention to the structure of your sentences. Remember what you have learned about sentence length, periodic and loose sentences, voice, and parallelism. Rewrite any passages that could be improved to achieve greater clarity, economy, or emphasis.

## Sounds and Rhythms

Think about the sounds of our language for a minute. Why should the combined English sounds of *d* plus *o* plus *g* have to signify an animal with four legs? Writers, like other people, tend to take this arbitrary relationship for granted.

Sometimes the sounds of words are directly related to their meaning. The sounds of *d* plus *o* plus *g* may not directly signify or even suggest the idea of *dog*. On the other hand, a combination of sounds like *s, w, i, s, h* can directly suggest the idea of a "hissing movement" which is what the word *swish* means. Or the sounds in a phrase like "the tin-pan tinkling of a rinky-dink piano" can directly reinforce the meaning. A serious writer uses the sounds of language to good advantage.

# Alliteration

Sometimes the placement of a single repeated sound can create a special effect. Can you complete this line: "Peter Piper picked a peck of..."? It's probably been some time since you recited that tongue twister, but you probably completed it correctly without any problem. Sentences constructed in this manner tend to be easy to recall. This repetition of like sounds at the beginning of words in a phrase or sentence is called *alliteration*. Children enjoy alliteration, especially when it's used in excess as in "Peter Piper." Writers can use it to good effect in a more controlled way. Notice how Robert Coffin uses it in these two paragraphs taken from his essay, *"Whistling Wings."*

**"Doubtlessly God could have made a better berry than the strawberry," said a seventeenth-century philosopher and friend of Izaak Walton, but doubtlessly God never did. The same applies to Merrymeeting among the bays famed for duck shooting. There might have been better places to shoot wild ducks in this wide green world, but they don't exist, glory be to God!**

**When the stars are at their highest, and the cocks still in the depths of sleep, all male Merrymeeting souls go out by lanternlight to the bay. The frost is pretty sure to be sifted by this time. The men and boys walk through the dust of diamonds. The last pale frostflowers crumble under their feet. Pines loom larger than life among the stars.**

How many alliterated phrases are used in the first paragraph? Think about the purpose of this paragraph. Does this very limited use of alliteration seem appropriate here?

The use of alliteration in the second example is increased. Note how it helps establish a relationship between emphasis and meaning.

Used well, alliteration has a powerful but subtle effect. Used in excess, it can be ineffective, even silly. Suppose the author had formed his last line to read, "Lengthy pines loom larger than life among the livid stars"? Aren't you glad he didn't?

Alliteration can occur by accident in writing. Since it suffers easily from overuse, you should employ it in a conscious and controlled manner. Save it for key descriptive passages where it will add the most to your writing.

## Talking Words, or Onomatopoeia

Use of a word whose sound directly suggests its meaning is called onomatopoeia. The word *swish* referred to earlier is an example.

Onomatopoeia can enhance your descriptive writing if, like other techniques, it is aptly applied and not overused. Onomatopoeia is a fairly obvious technique. This means you should not *"Zap"* or *"Pow"* your reader at every turn. Not every steak has to "sizzle" and not every bee has to "buzz." Use onomatopoeia naturally but sparingly.

## We've Got Rhythm. . .

A good writer can use the rhythm as well as the sounds of language to advantage. Since rhythm is both a part of nature and a part of language, writers can frequently use one to reflect the other. If the object or scene being described has a natural rhythm, the writer can often communicate the appropriate sensations through the rhythmic use of language as well as the meanings of words. For example, see how Henry Beston captures the eternal rhythms of the sea in this quotation.

Another thundering, and the water that has escaped and withdrawn is gathered up and swept forward again by another breaking wave. Night and day, age after age, so works the sea, with infinite variation obeying an unalterable rhythm moving through an intricacy of chance and law.

This paragraph describes the overall rhythm of the sea, one of breaking and gathering. Note how the structure of the last sentence in the quotation helps convey this endless, two-part rhythm.

Passages such as this sea scene are not unusual. You too can use the cadences of language to reinforce the natural rhythms of almost any moving object: falling rain, bouncing basketballs, wind-blown trees, or diesel engines. What is sometimes more difficult is to use rhythmic patterns to complement a deliberate tone or mood in your writing. Read these two contrasting passages carefully to see how the sentence structure in each reinforces the sounds of the words. Each is the opening to a famous short story by Edgar Allan Poe. The first is from *"The Fall of the House of Usher"* and the second from *"The Tell-Tale Heart."*

During the whole of a dull, dark, and soundless day in the autumn of the year, when the clouds hung oppressively low in the heavens, I had been passing alone, on horseback, through a singularly dreary tract of country; and at length found myself, as the shades of the evening drew on, within view of the melancholy House of Usher.

True!—nervous—very, very dreadfully nervous I had been and am; but why will you say that I am mad? The disease had sharpened my senses—not destroyed—not dulled them. Above all was the sense of hearing acute. I heard all things in the heaven and in the earth. I heard many things in hell. How, then, am I mad? Hearken! and observe how healthily—how calmly I can tell you the whole story.

In the first excerpt, Poe uses several techniques to establish a gloomy, ominous mood. First is his use of setting. Note the time of year, the time of day, and the place. How do the sounds of the words he uses in this description contribute to the mood?

Read this first passage aloud. Notice how the rhythmic structure reinforces the mood. The images come to you in wave after wave of depression. Unlike Beston's description of the sea, this rhythm is not natural to the scene. Poe has deliberately superimposed it, to suggest artificially but effectively an overwhelming sense of inevitable doom, the inevitable fall of the House of Usher.

The second excerpt from Poe is quite different. What statements directly indicate that the person telling the story is mad? What statements indirectly suggest this conclusion?

What disjointed rhythmic patterns does Poe employ to help convey this impression of madness?

To write in a manner which clearly expresses your meaning is not always easy. You must be aware of all the complexities of word meaning and grammar. In addition, you should try to pay attention to the sounds of your words and the rhythms of your sentences. Make them support what you are saying. The effects they achieve can be powerful. Sounds and rhythm can be somewhat like the background music in a film. Background music can affect viewers who may not consciously be aware of its presence.

The same is true of sounds and rhythms in writing. They will affect your readers, even if the readers do not consciously think about them.

# Things to Do

Choose one of the following topics or pick one of your own. Write a description using some of the sound and rhythm techniques discussed in this chapter. Concentrate on those techniques which you feel will best get across your meaning. Don't try to use them all in one paragraph.

**a high wind**
**a soft or violent rain viewed through a window**
**a blizzard or soft snowfall viewed through a window**
**a noisy machine**
**a powerful, smooth-running machine**
**a fire**
**a waterfall**
**a professional or experienced athlete performing**
**a skilled craftsman at work**

Go back and pick a different topic on which to write. Try to select one that will give you practice in at least one different technique from what you used in the last paragraph.

Share descriptions you just wrote with one or more members of your class. See if they can recognize the techniques you employed. Are there improvements that could be made? If so, rewrite the paragraph.

Copy your revised descriptions into your journal for future reference.

*When I have no idea, I gnaw my nails and invoke the aid of Providence.*

Brander Matthews

*I began to wonder about this time just what one saw when one looked at anything, really looked at anything.*

Gertrude Stein

*To put a sentence together is like climbing a mountain range. I really mean it.*

Wilbur Steele

*Proper words in their proper places . . .*

Jonathan Swift

*One writes from one thing only —one's experience.*

James Baldwin

# Chapter 5

# Developing a Plot

Story telling goes back to the time of the parable and the fable, to the time when blind bards sang their songs of superheroes—back even to the story of Cain and Abel. Back perhaps to the very beginning of time.

All stories, since the beginning, have been based upon the relation of a series of events. So, let's begin with a series of events. Study this list of events carefully.

# Conflict: The Heart of the Matter

1. Arguing with parents over going to New York to visit my brother.
2. Deciding to run away.
3. Getting up early and sneaking out of the house.
4. Waiting in darkness at the bus depot.
5. Meeting a new friend on the bus.
6. Stopping for lunch at Tarrytown on the Hudson River.
7. Arriving at the bus station in New York.
8. Walking through crowded streets.
9. Visiting the Empire State Building.
10. Walking through Central Park.
11. Getting lost.
12. Stopping at a tavern for directions.
13. Arriving finally at my brother's rooming house and finding him gone.
14. Eating supper in a dirty restaurant.
15. Waiting in darkness for my brother's return.
16. Talking with a policeman who stopped to question me.
17. Seeing my brother getting out of a car with friends.

What has determined the order in which the events in this series are listed?

Try rearranging some of the events in this list. Are there some that could be rearranged without really changing the sequence? Could some events be dropped from the list without losing too much?

All of the events involve the same individual. Do any of them focus primarily on some other topic or subject?

The list of events reflects an experience. Does the list provide any interpretation of this experience?

This list of events is a simple, unplotted narrative. What makes it "unplotted"? It provides no selection, no focus on a particular problem, no pattern other than time sequence, and no interpretation. A simple narrative, in this sense, merely reflects life as it is experienced.

In order to create literature which interprets human experience, a writer must select and arrange events to form a preconceived, carefully structured pattern. Moreover, this pattern must also reflect the interplay of one force against another, so that a conflict or problem is developed, climaxed, and finally resolved in a manner that reveals some truth about human experiences. This patterning of events is called a plotted narrative, or simply a plot. *Plot,* then, is the means by which a story is structured, and *conflict* is the essence of the plot.

The list of events you have just read represents an unplotted narrative. However, it would be possible to work this list into a story line, a brief synopsis or single paragraph summary of a plotted narrative. Think about constructing such a story line. Which events would you include? Which would you develop? Which would you leave out? How can you make these decisions? First determine what kind of conflict you want your story to present. Then structure a series of events to develop that conflict, and only that conflict.

Since literature generally deals with the conflicts of people, part of your decision is easy. In working with the above list of events, whatever conflicts you choose would involve the person to whom all of the events happened. Let's assume he's a boy named Alan.

Suppose you wanted to create a conflict out of the fact that Alan has an argument with his parents. What subsequent events would you choose to develop this conflict? How would you have it reach a high point? How then would you resolve it in such a way that Alan and the reader would learn about or be reminded of a significant aspect of life? The exact nature of the conflict and the events selected to structure it would be up to each writer producing the story. This particular conflict represents the first general type of conflict, *person versus person.*

Or, in looking over the list of events, you might decide that a good plot could be developed out of Alan's confrontation with New York City. The city's physical size, its social aloofness, its varied life styles could all present problems quite different from the issues of a family quarrel. Which events might contribute most significantly to the development of such a conflict? How could the conflict be resolved in a meaningful fashion? This particular kind of conflict would represent a second general type, *person versus society.*

Not all story conflicts, however, are people against people. A person can be pitted against one or more elements of nature as well. Adventure stories often use this approach. Heroes can fight off animals, climb mountains, cross deserts, or battle the elements, thereby demonstrating something about human nature. What aspects of nature does Alan encounter? Could you design a plot structured around such a conflict that would be an intense and meaningful adventure tale? What events would you select? This third type of conflict is *person versus nature*.

If Alan is not going to do battle with other people or nature, there's one type of conflict left for him. That conflict is a struggle with himself. This fourth general type of conflict, *person versus self,* is not quite as easy to develop from the list of events as were the other three types. But, it can be done. For example, what problems might Alan have to resolve within himself as a result of having run away? Are there any temptations that might have to be struggled with as a result of a frustrating day in the city? Any fears? What events might you use to bring about a resolution of this struggle within Alan, the main character, or protagonist, as the main character is called?

As you consider the various types of conflict, keep two points in mind. One is that a short story usually presents only one type of conflict at a time. Some forms of literature (generally those of greater length) may present more than one type, but a short story should be short. Its plot must hold together, which for now means restricting it to the development of a single conflict: a person versus some other element.

Also, as you plan conflict for your story, remember the old adage, "Truth is stranger than fiction." Sometimes it's too strange. When a story idea comes to you, test it for plausibility. Is it likely to have happened? If not, keep looking. Of course, events can take a sudden turn and coincidences do occur. But don't overdo such gimmicks. Don't push your reader's willingness to believe too far. For example, the events in the following account from *Time* magazine really did happen, but you might have trouble making a reader of fiction believe it.

**On Feb. 12, 1973, a pickup truck traveling on an Alabama highway at high speed went round a curve, spun out of control, and turned over into a ditch. The driver, Kenneth R. Barton, lay helpless, bleeding from an artery. State Trooper Kenyon M. Lassiter happened by in his patrol car and quickly applied a tourniquet. He eventually got Barton safely to a hospital, and was credited with saving his life.**

Not long ago, Trooper Lassiter stood by the side of a car he had stopped and was writing the driver a ticket when a pickup truck swerved across the road, struck the car Lassiter had stopped, and killed the trooper as he tried to duck behind his patrol car. The pickup truck bounced off the patrol car and kept on going. The next day the truck's driver turned himself in to the Covington County sheriff. He admitted he had been out the night before visiting several bars, but was unable to remember going home or who drove the truck. He was later charged with manslaughter and leaving the scene of an accident. The truck turned out to be the same one involved in the 1973 accident, and it also had the same driver: Kenneth R. Barton.

## Things to Do

Go back to your journal and find a simple narrative of an incident you witnessed or an experience you had. Using this passage as a starting point, write a list of events with at least 15 items. Keep the list in chronological order and add events that you think would be appropriate even though they may not have been a part of the original experience. Only add those events that you know about or can describe in detail.

Study the list of events you've just written. Try to identify at least two of the four types of conflict described in this chapter.

1. **person vs. person**
2. **person vs. society**
3. **person vs. nature**
4. **person vs. self**

After finding at least two of the four types of conflict, jot your conflicts down along with any plot development or resolutions that come to mind. Talk to your teacher or classmates about what you've done and see if it makes sense. If the consensus is that your idea would not work or be meaningful, look again at your list. Try again. Perhaps you will need to write a new list based on a different situation.

## Looking at the Whole

You already know that some form of conflict is essential to a story. You know that a plot must be structured so that it introduces the conflict, develops the conflict logically to a high point, and finally resolves it. Very simply, this means that every story must have a beginning, a middle, and an end, with each section developing certain aspects of the story.

The beginning must introduce the setting, the characters, and the conflict, though not necessarily in that order. Setting will include both time and place. Place is normally more important and would, therefore, be more fully described. Neither aspect should be described beyond its direct relationship to the characters and plot. In other words, don't tell more about the time and place than your readers need to know.

Characters, too, must be introduced. They may be described separately, or, in order to show important relationships among them, the author may present the characters interacting within a group. Tell enough so that the characters can be visualized and their motives understood. Don't tell so much that the development or movement of the plot is seriously delayed.

Introduce or hint at the conflict as soon as possible. How specific to be depends on the type of conflict to be developed. Usually the beginning of the story will present an *initial incident,* an event that creates a sense of instability. This initial incident indicates that something is wrong by revealing who is opposing what or whom, and suggesting why.

The middle of the story proceeds from the initial incident, and develops the conflict through a series of closely related and seemingly natural incidents called the *rising action*. By using related incidents instead of one uninterrupted experience, the author can allow the plot to rise and fall, each time reaching greater heights of intensity. Eventually, this building and releasing of the rising action has gone as far as it can, and the story reaches a structural turning point, a *crisis,* where the opposing forces interlock in some decisive action. For some readers, this point may also represent the climax of the story, the peak of excitement or highest emotional response. In some stories or for other readers, the climax may come later toward the end of the story.

The end must move quickly to present the *falling action,* the unraveling of the plot, and thus the resolution of the conflict. Since much must be accomplished within this relatively small section, the ending of a story is a test of its unity. Everything must be tied together, be explained, or seem reasonable without drawing the story out to where it becomes anticlimactic or boring.

In addition to these structural requirements, the ending of a story must also reveal the theme of the work. The ending should suggest a central idea—some meaningful concept about the nature of life or the nature of people. The theme is rarely stated directly. It should be revealed naturally from the order of events presented by the author. It should be something that readers can determine for themselves. Authors of fables or parables can preach or moralize, but as a short story writer you should allow your readers to draw their own conclusions.

## A Lively Story

Here's a chance to read a story and see how it works. Read the following short story by Jean Lively, who wrote it as a sixteen-year-old high school student. First read it for pleasure. Don't look at the notes as you read. Then read it again. The notes will help you analyze its structure so you can apply some of these techniques to your own writing.

## The Flight of the Snowbird

*A FIRST AWARD—SENIOR SHORT STORY in the 1965 Scholastic Magazines Writing Awards sponsored by the W. A. Sheaffer Pen Co.*

**By Jean Lively, 16**
**South High School**
**Denver, Colorado**
**Teacher, Margaret McIntosh**

[1]  *The snow was falling quickly now. It was beginning to form little piles in the corners of the wooden cross of the window pane. The winter sky was pink-white and the bare trees in the front yard cast their weird shadows in the pale winter light.*

[2]  *Suddenly something flapped its way into the yard. It landed awkwardly in the snow and fell forward on its beak. The bird struggled to its feet and glanced around intently. It was small and white, about the size of a sparrow. The bird waddled around clumsily, occasionally pecking at the ground.*

[3]  *The boy at the window watched the bird with his nose against the glass. He pressed his forehead against the pane and then watched as its vapor print disappeared. He did this three times and wondered if he would be able to get away from them tonight. The lawn chairs in the front yard were heavy with snow and he longed to be outside and tip them over.*

[4]  *His mother called him and the bird flew off. The boy watched it fly gracefully across the moonlit sky and idly wondered to himself what kind of bird it was. He watched it until it was out of sight behind the barn and then resumed his drawings on the window.*

[5]  *His mother called him again sharply, and he began to walk slowly through the hall and out to the kitchen. He stepped into the warmly heated sun porch and waited. Without looking up from the table his mother said, "Go wash your hands in the kitchen." The boy frowned but went into the kitchen and swished his hands through the cold water. Waving them dry, he walked back to the sun porch.*

[6]  *While his mother said grace he drew designs on the worn oilcloth with his fingernail. He picked up his spoon and dipped it into the steaming chicken noodle soup.*

[7]  *"Don't lean on the table, Son." His mother said this softly. The boy frowned but took his elbows off the table. Crumbling a cracker into his soup, he forced his eyes over to where his sister was sitting. Her eyes were already fastened on his face. Could she read his mind? Sometimes it seemed to him that she saw right through him.*

[8]  *A wet noodle was pasted against her chin and he looked away in disgust as his mother helped the noodle back into her mouth and tried to get her to start eating again.*

[9]  *He finished eating his soup and drank his milk in one gulp. "Can I go now?" His mother looked up, puzzled. "Where?"*

[10]   The boy frowned at her impatiently as if she should know. "I thought I'd go out to the pond and try my new skates."

[11]   His mother glanced over to where his sister sat and said softly, "Wait a few minutes and you can take her with you."

[12]   The boy pushed his chair violently and said loudly, "I'm going by myself. I won't take her."

[13]   "Please, Benjy, you never give her a chance. You know how she loves to skate. Just because she can't tell you, you think you can ignore her. Please let her go with you this time."

[14]   The boy was watching the curious noodles left in his soup bowl. He mumbled something. His mother looked up and said, "What did you say?"

[15]   "I said it's impossible to ignore her. She always stares at me. I'm not taking her."

[16]   A strand of gray hair fell across his mother's pale cheek and she said tiredly, "Her skates are in the hall closet."

[17]   The boy stared at both of them with hate and then burst out, "I won't take her!" He ran to the closet and grabbed his coat, mittens, and cap. Slamming the door behind him, he ran stiff-legged to the shed and opened the creaky door. He looked over to where his skates hung. Their bluish blades were glittering in the pale light. He pulled them off the peg and felt their sharp blades against his palm. Touching the soft black leather and silver eyelets, he slung them across his shoulder and ran into the yard. The lawn chairs were still waiting and he went over to them and tipped each one over. He smiled and ran across the field.

[18]   The skates thumped gaily against his back, and he looked around the pasture to see it was almost as light as daytime outside. The winter moonlight gave everything an unnatural glow and made the trees and bushes stand out darkly against the snow.

[19]   The snow was still falling but more lightly now, and he let it tickle his nose until his eyes began to water; then he scratched at his nose furiously. The snow beneath his feet was soft and his shoes squeaked crisply.

[20]   At the end of the pasture, the pond gleamed brightly like an open eye. He sat down on a snow-covered hay rake and put on his skates. Tying the shoelaces of his other shoes, he slung them across his back and walked to the edge of the pond. He stood there and shivered deliciously.

[21]   *Something tugged at his coat and his stomach jumped. He looked down to see his sister. Her coat was buttoned up crookedly and her muffler was tied loosely. He saw that her nose was running.*

[22]   *He reached into his pocket and pulled out a wadded up Kleenex and wiped her nose viciously. Taking her hand, he pulled her roughly over to the rake. As he sat her down he considered for a moment sending her back, but knew he would get in trouble if he did. He laced her skates too tight and looked to see if there was any change in her face, but there was none . . . nothing at all. Even when the laces bit into her skin, she sat looking at him, her eyes boring quietly through him.*

[23]   *"Why couldn't she have had a good baby instead of you?" He looked at her as if she were something loathsome and hated himself for hating her. She was nothing to him but a barrier between him and his mother. At times he found he couldn't even remember her name. But then, perhaps he made himself forget. He finished lacing her skates and then walked away from her.*

[24]   *There was a slight breeze now and it cut through his corduroy pants. He slid out onto the pond and began to skate. His ankles ached pleasantly, and he could feel his sharp blades hiss and scrape on the ice below the snow. The cold was numbing; it bit into his face and ears, making them tingle.*

[25]   *Skating backward, he could see her coming up behind. He watched her skate toward him with a gracefulness he knew he would never have. She was a good skater, he admitted. But did she really know what she was doing? Was skating just something that came naturally to her? She wasn't well coordinated with her fingers but she could skate better than anyone he knew. Maybe it was her smallness and frailness that made her so detestable to him. So pale and white.*

[26]   *He watched her slide across the pond like a piece of chipped ice. Then he turned around and skated forward. He stopped to sniff his nose and felt a gentle tug at his coat. He shook her loose and went the other way.*

[27]   *He used to have his friends over, but she would stand behind the kitchen door and stare at them, until they stopped coming altogether. She made them feel uneasy.*

[28]   *She could tell if he was happy, and if he was she would pad along behind him and hang on to his shirttail. But always*

*there were the eyes following him around. Empty eyes boring through his back when he wasn't looking.*

*[29]   He looked around for her and couldn't see her. He skated to the middle of the pond and looked around. Then he saw her over on the part of the pond that was off limits to them. There was no sign, but he knew it was thin ice.*

*[30]   For a moment he stood motionless. It would be so easy. So easy to tell his mother he hadn't even known she was there . . . so easy to see the look of age and weariness disappear from her lined face . . . no more kind and patient words from his sister's bedroom, no more look of defeat on his mother's face when his sister wouldn't learn to tie her own shoes. There would be no more tears from his mother.*

*[31]   He watched as his sister slid farther and farther away. Suddenly he saw something out of the corner of his eye. It was the small awkward bird that flew so beautifully. It was flying slowly across the pond but when the boy looked at it directly it disappeared; but he knew it was there. He had seen it.*

*[32]   His legs began to pump forward and his skates dug frantically at the ice. He couldn't see her now and his legs were burning with impatience. He swung his arms to try to get up speed. He couldn't seem to move fast enough, and tears were beginning to stream from his eyes. She was visible to him now. He watched as she skated onto the thin part. Then he heard the loud crack and he felt the ice tremble and shake. He edged carefully to the hole in the ice and grabbed the tail of her coat. He clung tight as the ice water numbed his fingers. Pulling as hard as he could, he saw her head appear. The coat slipped from his fingers and he lost her. Desperately he thrust both arms into the water and searched frantically for her. He felt her coat in his hands again, and this time he heaved her out onto the ice.*

*[33]   For what seemed a long time he watched her blue face and prayed for her eyes to open. His stomach jerked convulsively when her eyes opened. She began to shiver and he quickly took off her clothes; he laid her on his warm coat and wrapped it around her small body. He was vaguely aware of his freezing arms and hands as he took off his skating socks and put them on her feet. The biting cold cut into his feet and he tried but couldn't unlace his other shoes. He slipped them on as best he could. Picking her up he started to walk to the edge of the pond. Her body was very still in his arms and he noticed her lips were cut*

and bleeding. He took the tissue from his pocket and wiped the blood away. Looking down at her face he searched for something in her eyes but still there was nothing . . . no pain, no accusation, nothing . . . except tears. Never before had he seen her cry. Even when his mother would cry her heart out in front of his sister, she would sit and stare unknowingly. Now the tears began to form and roll down her cheeks. The boy finally remembered her name. It was Sheryl. She struggled closer to the warmth of his body and unconsciously he hugged her closer to him. Looking at her he softly said her name. At last he saw something more than emptiness. He saw that she recognized him. He began to walk faster.

## Structuring a Story Beginning

In the first two paragraphs of the story, the author presents part of the setting. The paragraph reveals the time of year and tells us something about the setting in which the story takes place. The second paragraph introduces a very specific and appropriate part of that season, a snowbird. What additional aspects of setting could the author have revealed here? Notice that these details were withheld until later. Is this technique effective?

What other necessary description could the author have begun with other than setting?

Does the reader realize at this point why the snowbird is mentioned so prominently and described so thoroughly?

What characteristics of the bird does the author concentrate on? Does the reader know why?

Do you see now why Miss Lively chose to open with setting as opposed to some other description?

In the third paragraph, the author introduces the first character, a boy—no name, just *"the boy."* Can you think of any advantage to not naming the boy at this point?

Instead of describing the boy, the author describes the boy's actions. What advantage does a description of action have over a straight-forward explanation of a character?

What do the boy's actions reveal about his nature? Are his actions unusual?

What statement suggesting the upcoming conflict appears in the third paragraph? In what ways is the statement vague? Do you think the author purposely omitted certain details? Does this intensify the action later on?

The fourth paragraph returns to the setting by telling us more about the place and revealing the time of day. Then the next paragraph brings in a second character who was only mentioned by name in paragraph four. What does the boy's failure to respond to his mother's call tell you about him and his present attitude?

What also is revealed about the boy and his relationship to his mother by the way he responds to her command to wash his hands?

Paragraphs five and six reveal more of the setting. The author allows the detailed description to show us that the home is warm and comfortable but not prosperous. What specific details prompt these impressions?

Paragraphs seven and eight introduce the third and last character, the boy's sister, but again, without revealing her name. The paragraph also reveals the boy's attitude toward her. What is that attitude?

What effect is achieved by having the boy express his attitude nonverbally? He "looked away in disgust." Is this more effective than having him speak?

It's not unusual for brothers and sisters to have trouble getting along, but the attitude shown by this boy is too strong to pass as normal sibling rivalry. Something is very wrong—there is a major conflict. This scene therefore is the initial incident. So we have the setting, the characters, and the conflict, which are the requirements for the beginning of the story. How would you classify the type of conflict being suggested at this point—person versus person, society, nature, or self?

More must be told. The author goes on to show us the mother's tired attempt to promote understanding between the boy, whose name is now revealed, and his sister, who "can't tell" him how she "loves to skate." Loves to skate? A girl who is old enough to skate but still can't speak? Suddenly we recognize a reason for the conflict. Benjy rejects his sister because she's disabled. This realization prompts numerous questions which will have to be explained as the plot develops, but already the author has shown us a great deal.

The beginning of the story has accomplished what it was meant to do, as Benjy slams the door and walks out. Besides introducing the setting, characters, and conflict has the author succeeded in interesting the reader to read on? What would you consider to be the strengths and weaknesses of the beginning of Miss Lively's story? Does the omission of certain detail strengthen your interest? Or, should the author have included more detail? Not all readers will agree. As a writer these are decisions you will have to make for your readers.

To what extent did she present the setting, characters and initial incident as separate descriptions? To what extent did she blend these basic essentials?

Would it ever be possible to separate totally the three? Why?

What must you take into consideration in order to decide whether your opening lines should depict setting, character, or the initial incident?

Miss Lively closes her story's beginning and initial incident like this.

[17] **The boy stared at both of them with hate and then burst out, "I won't take her!" He ran to the closet and grabbed his coat, mittens, and cap. Slamming the door behind him. . . .**

Just for a moment, consider this possibility—consider the above lines as the opening to Miss Lively's story. What if these were the first words you had read? Imagining this possibility takes some re-thinking, but look at the passage carefully. If this had opened the story, to what extent would character have been revealed? To what extent would the conflict have been revealed? The setting?

Think about how the events which occurred prior to this scene could be included. Would they need to be? How would the beginning of the story be changed by all of this?

Obviously Miss Lively did not open her story in this manner. In the beginning she narrated events in a chronological order without having to go back into the past to bring us up to date. But had she used this alternative opening, she would have been employing a very useful technique which many stories do use. It's one you may want to consider in some of the stories you write. This technique is called a *flashback*.

Flashback is effectively used as a condensing technique. Thus in stories where significant events precede the point at which the author wishes to begin, the author briefly flashes back to the past to bring the reader up to date. For such stories, an alternative to flashback is a long account of preliminary events resulting in a lengthy, possibly boring, beginning.

However, the problem most beginning writers have with flashback is not in using it, but in moving effectively into it and out of it in a natural manner. People don't usually recall the past without reason. Something normally triggers it, some sensory impression which they associate or remember—a picture, a person, a sound, a smell: almost anything can have this effect. Likewise, such impressions can also be used to pull characters out of a flashback and return them to the present. Someone bumps them, a door slams, a light flashes, or something convenient happens to accomplish this.

Besides using flashback as a technique for condensing the time line of a story, what other advantages can you see for using it in terms of reader interest?

In your opinion, would Miss Lively's story have been more effective if she had used an initial flashback? Is it effective the way it is? An author of a short story cannot take time to tell everything that has happened in all of the characters' lives. As an author you will have to decide what scene to begin with and how much flashback, if any, is necessary. Miss Lively's story is one example of how this decision can be made.

## Things to Do

Even though we haven't worked yet with character and setting and these will affect the manner in which you begin your story, you might find it helpful to practice writing one or more story beginnings. You may use the conflict sketch you have already written as a basis for your beginning, or work with a new idea. Use a variety of methods for introducing setting, character, and initial incident.

Go back to the list of events involving Alan and practice writing a flashback. Open your narrative with a description of the fourth, fourteenth, or fifteenth event. Then provide a means for Alan to recall the argument with his parents which led him to run away, and finally bring him out of the flashback into the present again.

Read several short stories to see how various authors begin to establish the setting, character and initial incident. How is the conflict presented? For those stories using flashback, notice what sensory devices are used to move into and out of the recall.

If you don't have any stories in mind, you might try some of these:

**"Rip Van Winkle"** *by Washington Irving*
**"Silent Snow, Secret Snow"** *by Conrad Aiken*
**"Winter Dreams"** *by F. Scott Fitzgerald*
**"Soldiers' Home"** *by Ernest Hemingway*
**"The Eighty-yard Run"** *by Irwin Shaw*
**"The Lottery"** *by Shirley Jackson*
**"The Occurrence at Owl Creek Bridge"** *by Ambrose Bierce*
**"The Secret Life of Walter Mitty"** *by James Thurber*

## Structuring the Middle

**Slamming the door behind him, he ran stiff-legged to the shed and opened the creaky door.**

This sentence opens the middle section of "The Flight of the Snowbird." Here five related incidents will develop the rising action to a decisive structural peak. The first incident begins with the above quoted sentence and runs through paragraph twenty. Read it again if you need to.

The author sets off the beginning of the story from the middle. Notice how this is done with a break in the physical setting. Along with this physical break there's a change in Benjy's mood. What is it? What specific actions show this?

Quietly but abruptly, incident number two breaks this new mood and brings the conflict back to Benjy as his sister softly tugs at his coat. He hasn't escaped after all, so now the conflict can be moved another step forward. Again the details reveal what we need to know. How does the business of wiping her nose express the cross-current, almost self-contradictory attitudes within Benjy?

How does he attempt to vent his frustration on her?

Then in paragraph twenty-three, Benjy voices his feelings directly to her for the first time. *"Why couldn't she have had a good baby instead of you?"* A *"good"* baby? Not a *"healthy"* or *"normal"* baby, but a *"good"* baby! Does this statement deepen the conflict? How?

Why is it significant that Benjy spoke this feeling rather than simply thinking it to himself?

Then other feelings are revealed. How does Benjy indicate that his relationship with his mother has been affected by his feelings toward his little sister? "At times," Benjy "can't even remember her name." What do you think this means?

Incident number three, which starts with paragraph twenty-four, gives us a surprise. We find out not only that the little girl can skate, but that she is very good at it—better even than Benjy. But the surprise is also significant, since every fact must move the story forward. The author's description of her and Benjy's reactions deepen the conflict even further. How? Which of his impressions of her seem to reveal that Benjy considers the child to be something less than human?

Beginning with paragraph twenty-seven, incident four briefly develops the "barrier" aspect of the conflict. What additional behavior does the child represent to Benjy here? Then within this same incident, the conflict is tightened one more notch. Conflict is based upon opposing forces. Irony, too, involves the use of opposites. Irony therefore often lends a poignant or even bitter touch to human conflict. There's an irony here concerning the brother's and sister's individual abilities to perceive and understand each other's moods. What is it?

The last incident in the middle section begins with paragraph twenty-nine. Note that the author again creates a physical break to set this incident off from the others. This physical break sets off the incident as a structural unit and injects a physical element into the conflict as well. His sister now is in danger, and Benjy, for the first time, sees a possible solution to his problem. It would be "so easy" to let her become physically and permanently lost.

Then suddenly the snowbird appears. The coincidence strains belief a bit, but it's necessary to the story. Why must Benjy see the bird at this precise moment? What structural purpose does this placement serve?

The author seems to hint that Benjy might have only imagined seeing the bird. Why do you think she does this?

The conflict has now been developed as far as possible. We've watched it grow from Benjy's peevish desires to go skating without his sister, to a half-formed wish for her death. This wish can now be either canceled or fulfilled by an act of Benjy's own choosing. We're ready now for the crisis, or climax, and the author does not disappoint us. The crisis comes in a single, fast-moving, suspenseful paragraph, number thirty-two.

## Cliffhangers and Coincidence

One of the most noticeable qualities of the crisis in Miss Lively's story is her use of suspense. We wonder first if Benjy will get to his sister in time to prevent her going through the ice. He doesn't. Then we wonder if he can save her. He tries. He catches her. He loses her. Finally, he succeeds. He drags her onto the ice. Through it all the suspense has kept our attention.

Notice the sentence length within the crisis paragraph. Such sentences help create a sense of rapid movement in the action. Why is rapid movement important to a crisis? Note that the crisis is not split among several paragraphs. This also helps achieve the sense of speed.

Suspense is a customary part of crisis, especially if the action between the opposing forces is climactic or violent. Suspense may also be used in parts of a story other than the crisis. The quiet building of a conflict, for example, can involve suspense too. Suspense in a story should hold the reader's interest. To do this it must also be believable. Incredible coincidence and miracles can be a bit too much.

# Things to Do

Go back to one or more of the stories you read at the end of the last unit. Trace the development of the conflict throughout the rising action. Notice the types of incidents the author uses to achieve a unified and logical sequence. Is suspense used to good advantage? Do the crisis and the climax occur at the same point?

Go back and look again at the story beginnings you have already written. Based on what you now know about rising action and development of conflict, choose one of your beginnings and develop a story line. Briefly sketch a series of events which could lead to a logical crisis. For now, limit your sketch to one paragraph and write it in the present tense.

# Structuring the End: Unraveling and Resolving

**[33]  For what seemed a long time he watched her blue face and prayed for her eyes to open.**

This line is the beginning of the end of the story. This final section presents the falling action, and a resolution to the conflict. Though the falling action must be brief, it must accomplish a lot. It must let us down gently, tie everything together, and give us something to think about. Miss Lively manages to do this all in one concise paragraph.

The first major purpose of the falling action is to lessen tension after the emotional impact of the climax or crisis.

As Benjy watches his sister revive, for the first time in his life he attempts to comfort her. Finally, he is rewarded. How does she respond to his attention and care? Relief, as a vital part of the falling action, has been provided. In other stories, of course, the relief might be presented differently. It may be comic or humorous, expected or ironic, sad or poignant, but in all cases it must be logical. What would you call the kind of relief provided by Miss Lively in "Snowbird"? Would a comic or humorous relief scene have been as appropriate?

Naturally, not every aspect of the conflict as it was developed needs now to be "unraveled," but crucial problems must be resolved. Miss Lively concentrates on three: the girl's previous inability to cry, the boy's inability to remember her name, and the lack of expression in her eyes. What actions resolve each of these three aspects of the conflict? Which of the three resolutions is related to the mother's involvement in the conflict?

Considering the nature of the total conflict, especially Benjy's previous view of his sister as being something less than human, which of the three resolutions would you view as most important to the success of the conclusion? Why?

How would you summarize the resolution of the story?

What is the purpose of the last line in the story?

# Sentiment: Don't Overdo It

In portraying any part of a story, but especially the ending, an author must be careful not to deal in excessive sentiment. You cannot beg the reader to feel for your characters. Show emotion, if it's a natural part of the story, but don't tell it. Skip terms like *pitifully, joyfully, tragically,* or *gratefully* in your description. Such expressions create sentimentality, which can detract from the portrayal of honest emotion. Instead, let the actions of a character speak for themselves. In that way, the readers can form feelings toward the characters on their own. Don't impose your feelings upon them.

Let your readers draw their own conclusions. How does this create greater interest in a story than if the author tells all?

What emotions does Miss Lively portray in her final paragraph? What specific actions reveal each of these emotions within Benjy and Sheryl? What types of sentimental expressions would have been less effective had they been used?

## What Does It All Mean?

A plot must be structured so it accomplishes everything you've studied so far. It should introduce basic elements, move sequentially toward a climax, and resolve quickly while expressing natural emotion. One other ingredient is needed as well. That ingredient is a theme, a significant human concept or idea behind the story.

Author and critic, Walter Havinghurst, explained the function of theme this way.

**A short story is an exploration of a point of interest in the course of experience. In the flow of life there are unhurried currents and slowly gathering tides. The short story cannot trace these deliberate movements with the complex play of forces—physical, social, and psychological—that hasten and retard them. But there are points at which experience rises to some crest of interests, like the crest of a sea; here is the moment of the short story. It deals with a point of experience that is crucial and revealing.**

**The short story, then, is experience portrayed so as to reveal its meaning. Truth is implicit in the story's action, lurking in it, accompanying it like a shadow. The story is a sharply focused glimpse of experience—warm, alive, and urgent. But the picture of life is not complete without its implicit meaning.**

Read Havinghurst's last line again. Notice that he says *"implicit meaning"*—implicit, not explicit. In other words, a story must have meaning but the author does not come out and overtly tell that meaning to the readers. Fiction writers let us learn from their stories the way we learn from life. We experience, and then draw our own conclusions.

What do you think is the theme of *"The Flight of the Snowbird"?* The story doesn't come right out and tell you, but it does give clues.

Think about the story and see if you can write the theme in a sentence or two. Then compare what you have written with what others in the class perceive as the theme.

Besides the nature of the conflict, the title of a story can sometimes be a key element to interpreting the theme. In *"The Flight of the Snowbird,"* the author uses a specific object, the snowbird, to serve specific purposes. Although the snowbird is not absolutely vital to the structure of the plot, its presence in paragraph thirty-one does seem to prompt Benjy to move and save his sister. The snowbird is probably important to the theme, so we should look at the snowbird and its flight in some detail. When the snowbird is first introduced (paragraph two), what limited significance can the reader assign to it and to its actions at that point?

At what succeeding point in the story did you first make any association between the bird and the sister? What details within the descriptions of the bird and the girl help to reveal that association?

Before the crisis, when Benjy sees the bird at the pond, is it significant that the bird is flying and not sitting still? Why?

Think about the parallelism between the bird and the girl. Does it represent simply an intensifying element for the conflict? Is it an aid to characterization? Or, is it a literary symbol? To what extent can each of these purposes be defended?

What now is your final interpretation of the theme of *"Snowbird"?* Is the theme something that reminds you of the importance of a concept you already knew? Or, is the theme a concept you had not thought about before reading the story?

As you can see, story endings can be complex arrangements and need to be written with great care. In terms of structure, they serve as a final test of the unity of the story. The conflict must come to a logical conclusion without too many strings left hanging. In terms of meaning, the ending provides an insight into human existence. It can't be too vague but it shouldn't instruct in such detail that the reader has nothing to think about.

As you work on your own stories, you'll see how tough it is to write a good ending. Even if you envision a good ending to a story very early in the idea stage, you may find as you go along that it needs work. Don't be afraid to rework it until it's right.

# Things to Do

You analyzed the middles of various short stories at the end of the last unit. Look again at these stories to see how they are concluded. Here are some questions to think about. Is the unraveling complete and logical? Would you have resolved the conflict a different way? Did the author play upon your sentiments by expressing emotional reactions for you? Can you decide upon a theme for the story? If so, how does it reflect the conflict? Is the theme reflected in any way by the title?

You've already tried to write story beginnings and middles. Now try writing at least one ending for your story line, in full detail. Discuss your work with others to get their opinions on unity and significance.

*Words are tools which automatically carve concepts out of experience.*

T. S. Huxley

*You must look into people as well as at them.*

Lord Chesterfield

# Chapter 6

# Developing Voice and Point of View

Do you recognize any of these people? They all have one thing in common. They are among the most famous story tellers in literature. They are Huck Finn, David Copperfield, Dr. Watson, and the narrator in *"The Tell Tale Heart"* by Edgar Allan Poe. Try to imagine yourself listening to each of them telling you a story. Suppose you were blindfolded. Do you think you could tell one from the other?

Huck Finn is an uneducated boy living on the banks of the Mississippi River in Hannibal, Missouri in mid-nineteenth-century America. David Copperfield is a well educated, highly polished gentleman of late nineteenth-century England. Dr. Watson is a medical doctor living in early twentieth-century London. The narrator in *"The Tell Tale Heart"* is a madman. Think about how these characters would differ in the way each of them would tell his story.

It's important for a short story writer to think carefully about whose voice will tell the story. By this time you probably have developed a story line for the short story you are going to write. Now you should think about who is going to tell your story and what kind of voice he or she should have—baker? banker? merchant? thief? doctor? lawyer? Indian chief? Yourself? Nobody?

In coming to a decision, you should answer two questions. "Who is going to tell my story?" and "How is my story going to get told?" This chapter will give you some help in answering these questions.

## The I's Have It

**I was born at Blunderstone, in Suffolk, or "thereby," as they say in Scotland. I was a posthumous child. My father's eyes had closed upon the light of this world six months when mine opened on it. There is something strange to me, even now, in the reflection that he never saw me; and something stranger yet in the shadowy remembrance that I have of my first childish associations with his white gravestone in the churchyard, and of the indefinable compassion I used to feel for it lying out alone there in the dark night, when our little parlour was warm and bright with fire and candle, and the doors of our house were—almost cruelly, it seemed to me sometimes—bolted and locked against it.**

This quotation is from the opening chapter of *David Copperfield*. It illustrates one of the basic ways to tell a story.

Who is telling the story? How do we know this?

From what point in time are the events of the story being told? Why do you suppose Dickens chose this particular point from which to view the events?

Can you think of some reasons to use the "*I*," the first person, to tell a story? Are there any disadvantages?

What do we learn, if anything, about the character of the "I" in this paragraph?

If the speaker were alive and telling his story directly, what do you think his voice would be like? Why? Reading the passage aloud may help you answer this.

Now, take a look at the following passage from *Daybreak* by Joan Baez.

Mimi and I were hanging around the Club 47 coffeehouse in Harvard Square. We were on the way home from Newport, '67. We were seeking old friends from eight years before, but also new faces, lots of new faces lined up in the warm New England evening. They let a blind girl in so she could find a seat. I watched the ticket lady hold her hand out timidly to return the change, not wanting to bump the blind girl's hand. When her things were in order the blind girl took the change and began calculating where she would sit, tapping a radar route around the tables and chairs. I went up to her and helped her find a seat.

"This is sort of comfy," I said, showing her the chair. "You're at the back, but on the aisle."

"Thank you very much," she said, sitting down and folding up her funny collapsible metal cane. Then she faced me and said, "Excuse me, but your voice sounds vaguely familiar. . ."

I told her my name and she let out a squeal.

"I'm Paula. Remember me? From Perkins? Gee, that was eight years ago! Gee, it's good to see you!"

From what point in time are the events being narrated? Can you guess which narrator, Joan Baez or David Copperfield, is probably closer to the events? Does this make a difference?

What does the passage reveal about the character of the narrator?

Compare the voice that speaks to you in this passage with that in the previous one. Point out specific ways in which each voice is established.

The first person point of view uses an "I" to tell the story. A story being told directly by a participant has immediacy. Some writers feel that the eye-witness account also provides more authenticity. Keep in mind, however, that in using this point of view you are limited to what the narrator sees, hears, and thinks. You cannot enter into the minds of other characters or present material that the narrator doesn't know. If you are considering a first person point of view for your story, also keep in mind that you must create a character whose background, mental characteristics, and attitudes will fit the way you want your story told. Remember the voice you create for your narrator must be consistent with his or her character and go along with the type of situation being presented. Joan Baez and David Copperfield are both telling the story of their past experiences, but can you imagine them changing places?

## See All, Know All, Tell All

Who is going to tell my story? How is it going to be told? One possible answer to these questions is to tell your story yourself, using the third person. This point of view permits the author to probe the minds of any of his or her characters, to move freely from one scene of action to another, and to comment, if desired, directly on any aspect of the story being told. Here are some passages from Hawthorne's *David Swan*. Read them carefully to see how a story can be told from the author's point of view.

**We can be but partially acquainted even with the events which actually influence our course through life, and our final destiny. . . . This idea may be illustrated by a page from the secret history of *David Swan*.**

**We have nothing to do with David until we find him, at the age of twenty, on the high road from his native place to the city of Boston, where his uncle, a small dealer in the grocery line, was to take him behind the counter. . . . After journeying on foot from sunrise till nearly noon of a summer's day, his weariness and the increasing heat determined him to sit down in the first convenient shade, and await the coming up of the stage-coach. As if planted on purpose for him, there soon appeared a little tuft of maples, with a delightful recess in the midst, and such a fresh bubbling spring that it seemed never to have sparkled for any wayfarer but David Swan. . . . The spring murmured drowsily beside him; the branches waved dreamily across the blue sky overhead; and a deep sleep, perchance hiding dreams within its depths, fell upon David Swan. But we are to relate events which he did not dream of.**

**He had slept only a few moments when a brown carriage, drawn by a handsome pair of horses, bowled easily along and was brought to a standstill in front of David's resting-place. A linchpin had fallen out, and permitted one of the wheels to slide off. The damage was slight, and occasioned merely a momentary alarm to an elderly merchant and his wife, who were returning to Boston in the carriage. . . .**

"How soundly he sleeps!" whispered the old gentleman. "From what a depth he draws that easy breath! Such sleep as that, brought on without an opiate, would be worth more to me than half my income; for it would suppose health and an untroubled mind."

"Providence seems to have laid him here," whispered she to her husband, "and to have brought us hither to find him, after our disappointment in our cousin's son. Methinks I can see a likeness to our departed Henry. Shall we waken him?"

"To what purpose?" said the merchant, hesitating. "We know nothing of the youth's character."

"That open countenance!" replied his wife, in the same hushed voice, yet earnestly. "This innocent sleep!"

While these whispers were passing, the sleeper's heart did not throb, nor his breath become agitated, nor his features betray the least token of interest. Yet Fortune was bending over him, just ready to let fall a burden of gold. The old merchant had lost his only son, and had no heir to his wealth except a distant relative, with whose conduct he was dissatisfied. In such cases, people sometimes do stranger things than to act the magician, and awaken a young man to splendor who fell asleep in poverty.

"Shall we not waken him?" repeated the lady persuasively.

"The coach is ready, sir," said the servant, behind.

The old couple started, reddened, and hurried away, mutually wondering what they should ever have dreamed of doing anything so very ridiculous. The merchant threw himself back in the carriage, and occupied his mind with the plan of a magnificent asylum for unfortunate men of business. Meanwhile, David Swan enjoyed his nap.

The carriage could not have gone above a mile or two, when a pretty young girl came along, with a tripping pace, which showed precisely how her little heart was dancing in her bosom. . . .

"He is handsome!" thought she, and blushed redder yet.

How could it be that no dream of bliss grew so strong within him, that, shattered by its very strength, it should part asunder, and allow him to perceive the girl among its phantoms? . . .

**"How sound he sleeps!"** murmured the girl.

**She departed, but did not trip along the road so lightly as when she came.**

Including David Swan, there are four characters in this portion of the story. In what passages does the author present the thoughts of each one? Could this have been accomplished by the use of any other viewpoint than that of the author?

Can you locate passages in which Hawthorne as author is commenting directly on the story he is telling? What is the effect of such comments?

Since no character in the story is the narrator, how is the voice established? How would you describe it? In what respects is it appropriate?

The point of view in which the author tells the story permits him or her to know all that occurs in the story. For this reason it is called the *omniscient* (all knowing) point of view. This point of view is the most flexible of all because it permits the author the greatest amount of freedom in telling the story. Used carefully, it can enable the author to present the story with breadth and depth of treatment. However, it must be used carefully. If the author intrudes needlessly into the story or moves too carelessly from one character's viewpoint to another's, the story won't ring true. In using the omniscient point of view, the hand of the author should not be seen pulling too many strings.

## To See, To Know, To Tell in Part

A third possibility in selecting a point of view for your story is to tell it in the third person but from the viewpoint of one character in the story rather than the viewpoint of the author. This is similar to the omnisicent point of view in that it employs the third person. It is different in that it limits the author to what the one character sees, hears, and thinks. The author can present in great depth the inner thoughts of this character, but cannot present the inner thoughts of any of the other characters.

Go back to *"The Flight of the Snowbird"* and reread it carefully. Pay particular attention to the way in which the writer uses point of view and voice.

Miss Lively uses the third person. From whose point of view is the story being told? Why do you suppose she selected this particular point of view? Would it be possible to tell the story from any other viewpoint?

If the author uses any character other than him or herself as the point of view, the character of that person must be revealed in the beginning of the story. At what point in "The Flight of the Snow-bird" do you feel that you have gotten to know Benjy? Describe his character and how it is revealed.

The writer cannot present the thoughts of either the mother or Sheryl. As a result, do we ever learn much about them?

As in the omniscient point of view, the author tells the story in the third person. In this case, however, it is limited to what *Benjy* sees, hears, and thinks. What determines the kind of voice an author will use?

One of the strengths of the limited third person point of view is that it permits you to tell your story as the character you use understands it. This is the case with Benjy. You must be careful, however, to create a voice that is appropriate to the character and to the situation. Don't simply speak in your own voice.

The third person limited point of view restricts what is told to what the one character sees, hears, and thinks. It sometimes creates problems for the inexperienced writer. Keep to what's believable. Try to avoid having your point-of-view character do things that don't make sense. Try to keep your point-of-view character from listening outside doors, eavesdropping on conversations, and accidentally being present whenever important events occur. Avoid having him or her get into things just for the purpose of telling the story. Make sure your readers can believe your point-of-view character. Don't force things.

## See Nothing, Know Nothing, Tell Nothing

A final possibility in deciding who is to tell your story and how it is to be told is, strangely enough, to have no one tell it at all. In other words, do not present your story from anyone's point of view, let it tell itself. Since no person's subjective viewpoint is involved, this is frequently called the *objective* point of view. Since it closely resembles the drama in its scenic method of presentation, it is sometimes called the *dramatic* point of view.

Using this point of view essentially places the author in the position of playwright and places the reader in the position of the viewer of the play. The reader sees and hears the characters but can only infer what they think and feel from what they say and do. The author becomes a kind of sound camera, may move about freely, but can record only what is seen and heard. This means that the author may set the scene and introduce characters, but then must tell the story largely by means of dialogue. For example, here is a selection from the opening of Hemingway's *"The Killers"*:

"I'll take ham and eggs," the man called Al said. He wore a derby hat and a black overcoat buttoned across the chest. His face was small and white and he had tight lips. He wore a silk muffler and gloves.

"Give me bacon and eggs," said the other man.

He was about the same size as Al. Their faces were different, but they were dressed like twins. Both wore overcoats too tight for them. They sat leaning forward, their elbows on the counter.

"Got anything to drink?" Al asked.

"Silver beer, bevo, gingerale," George said.

"I mean you got anything to *drink?*"

"Just those I said."

"This is a hot town," said the other. "What do they call it?"

"Summit."

"Ever hear of it?" Al asked his friend.

"No," said the friend.

"What do you do here nights?" Al asked.

"They eat the dinner," his friend said. "They all come here and eat the big dinner."

"That's right," George said.

"So you think that's right?" Al asked George.

"Sure."

"You're a pretty bright boy, aren't you?"

"Sure," said George.

"Well, you're not," said the other little man. "Is he, Al?"

"He's dumb," said Al. He turned to Nick. "What's your name?"

"Adams."

"Another bright boy," Al said. "Ain't he a bright boy, Max?"

"The town's full of bright boys," Max said.

The men are in a lunchroom. A few details of their appearance are recorded. The rest is dialogue. There is no point of view to provide interpretation. You have to interpret on your own. What impression do you get of the men in this scene?

The voice of a speaker in a drama reveals a phase of his personality. You as a viewer must pay attention not only to what is said but also to *how* it is said. How would you describe the voice of the speakers in this scene? Try reading the entire story. See if you can draw some conclusions about the way in which voice contributes significantly to the meaning of what is portrayed.

Since the author functions like a sound camera in recording only what is seen and heard, he must in the telling of the story rely heavily, as we have seen, upon dialogue and external action. One advantage of this is that the story moves more rapidly than if the author were presenting many expository passages and passages revealing the thoughts of the characters. Another advantage is that the reader must make his or her own interpretations and thus is more directly involved in the story. On the other hand, this point of view would not be effective in telling a story which presents an internal conflict because it relies so heavily on dialogue and external action. The objective point of view does not lend itself to depth in the treatment of character. It is also limited in that it doesn't move easily backward or forward in time.

We have just considered four points of view. Four different ways of seeing, knowing, and telling. Think of point of view as being literally a "point" from which you view and present your story. First of all, it is a "point" in time. You may, like David Copperfield, be telling of events that happened in the past. Or you may, like Huck Finn, be telling of events that are happening at the present time. The point of view is a "point" you establish not only in relation to time, but also in relation to your material. You may choose to view your story from the point of a first person, an omniscient author, a third person limited, or a point that is objective. As a writer, you must be careful to select the particular point of view which will best tell the story you have to tell.

Think of voice as being simply a representation of a phase or aspect of personality not through *what* is said but through *how* it is said. Keep in mind that the voice may be your own as author in the third person omniscient point of view, or it may be that of a separate and totally independent character that you create. Remember that the voice that speaks from your work must be appropriate to the person speaking and to the situation being presented.

In longer fiction, writers at times shift from one voice and point of view to another as their story demands. In shorter fiction, this is very difficult to do without destroying the unity of the work and its authenticity. So, in your short story you will probably do best if you carefully pick a point of view and stick to it.

## Things to Do

Go back to some of the short stories you have read. Look at each carefully to see what point of view the author uses. See if you can draw some conclusions as to why the author used that point of view. Look at the voice used. Pay particular attention to how it is created and whether it fits the point of view and the situation.

Read the Parable of the Good Samaritan in the New Testament. Any edition will do. Rewrite it from the point of view of:

**The Priest**
**The Levite**
**The Good Samaritan**

How do these stories differ? Which do you think is most effective?

By this time you should have developed a story line for your short story. You have probably done some experimenting with beginnings and endings and have been using one of the points of view in your experimenting. Now you should make a firm decision as to what point of view will be most effective in telling your story. Decide what voice might work best for the point of view and the situation presented in your story. It might help to jot down some notes and questions and discuss them with your teacher or with your friends. Look carefully at your story line, your experimental beginning and ending. See whether any changes or refinements are necessary for the voice and point of view you have selected.

# Chapter 7

## Developing Setting

Project yourself into each one of these scenes. What is your response to each? Are there differences from scene to scene? Why? Why not?

Stretch your imagination! Imagine *"The Fall of the House of Usher"* taking place in a ranch house in a modern suburb. Imagine *"Rip Van Winkle"* taking place in Central Park in New York City. Imagine *The Scarlet Letter* taking place in modern Boston. No? Why not?

Why would the Gothic architecture of Roderick Usher's ancestral home be more effective than the contemporary three-bedroom, bath-and-a-half ranch house? Why would the desolate, mist-shrouded landscape that surrounds it be more effective than the well-trimmed lawns of a modern suburb? Is the sleepy, magic atmosphere of the Catskills in the eighteenth century more appropriate for the setting of "Rip Van Winkle" than the tree-studded Central Park carousel and hot dog stands in the middle of New York City? Is colonial, Puritan Boston a more fitting locale for The Scarlet Letter than the traffic-burdened, cosmopolitan city of today? Why is the bleak, windswept beauty of the moors so appropriate for the setting of Wuthering Heights?

The associations that we have with certain settings, with kinds of landscape, with certain types of architecture, and with the historic past are somewhat mysterious, but they are real. Writers of all periods of time have made effective use of such associations. As far back as seventh or eighth-century England, the writer of Beowulf spoke of Grendel, the evil one, as dwelling in "the stretching moors and misty hollows."

Setting, in fiction, refers to the background against which the action takes place. We will distinguish three elements of setting:

1. **Place:  geographical location, and all physical features whether of a room, house, street, yard, city, landscape, seascape, sounds, smells, weather, etc.**

2. **Time:  period in historical time, time of day, day of the week, season of the year.**

3. **Human environment:  social, moral, religious, economic, and political conditions and customs; human occupations.**

As a writer, you must learn to use these elements of setting as effectively as possible. This chapter will show you some of the more important ways in which writers make use of setting.

## Setting the Stage

In the opening of James Baldwin's Another Country, Rufus is walking up Seventh Avenue in New York City. The following paragraph presents the scene through which he moves:

**The Avenue was quiet, too, most of its bright lights out. Here and there a woman passed, here and there a man; rarely, a couple. At corners, under the lights, near**

drugstores, small knots of white, bright, chattering people showed teeth to each other, pawed each other, whistled for taxis, were whirled away in them, vanished through the doors of drugstores or into the blackness of side streets. Newsstands, like small black blocks on a board, held down corners of the pavements and policemen and taxi drivers and others, harder to place, stomped their feet before them and exchanged such words as they both knew with the muffled vendor within. A sign advertised the chewing gum which would help one to relax and keep smiling. A hotel's enormous neon name challenged the starless sky. So did the names of movie stars and people currently appearing or scheduled to appear on Broadway, along with the mile-high names of the vehicles which would carry them into immortality.

You probably don't know well, if at all, the street Baldwin is describing. However, it must be obvious that he has selected only a few of the many physical details available to him in creating the scene. Why do you think he chose as he did?

These lines present a street scene in a large city. Does the setting create any particular mood or atmosphere? If not, what is the function of the setting?

Take a look at another setting. The following passage is from Gordon Parks' *The Learning Tree:*

The job started, Jack lit his pipe, rested his elbows on the window sill, and looked out over all Cherokee Flats from this perch. As he did, it came to him that the contours of the village resembled those of an egg, the broader top half representing where the most well-to-do resided, and the lower half being where the poor and near-poor lived. The Frisco tracks running north and south across the lower section, drew the social and economic line between the six thousand residents who made up the village. There were no well-to-do blacks, he reasoned, but there were poor whites who shared, to a certain degree, the status of their dark neighbors east of the tracks.

Far away on the north edge he could just see Flynn's River, the sun reflecting on its flat, slow-moving surface, snaking in and out of the craggy rocks and tall trees. Further beyond, where the water cut into the west, he saw the top of County Hospital that perched on a knoll on the very out-

**skirts of the village. He glanced toward the opposite end of the river where, off to the right of it, he recognized Jake Kiner's red farmhouse—barns, cattle pens and fruit orchards sprawling over the entire shank of the east hill. On up the gentle slopes the bright sun struck the white crosses and marble headstones marking the graves, and still further to the right of that the steep incline of candy hill down which the youth of Cherokee Flats raced their wagons and homemade vehicles in the summer, their sleds in the winter. All else outside the village perimeter, as far as he could see, was prairie, cornfield and brush.**

This scene presents a panoramic view of the little prairie town of Cherokee Flats, where much of the action of the novel takes place. What elements of setting are used?

Parks in no way could have included all of the physical details of the town. Can you suggest why he chose the ones he did?

In presenting a panoramic setting such as this one, the author must be careful to arrange the details so they create an orderly pattern. What arrangement has Parks employed? How do you think the author is using setting here?

These two settings present entirely different scenes but they are alike in illustrating an important function of setting in fiction. Fiction presents a significant human action, and no human action takes place in a vacuum. So, as a writer, you must present enough specific detail to create a sense of place. The amount of detail you present will depend upon the relative importance of setting to your story. In this sense, a basic use of setting is to set the stage for the action.

## Haunted Houses and Lovely Landscapes

People tend to have strong associations with certain aspects of their environment. So, you can use setting to evoke a mood or create an atmosphere ranging from the terror and mystery of the haunted house to the delight and repose of a lovely landscape. Here is a setting from *"The Fall of the House of Usher":*

**The room in which I found myself was very large and lofty. The windows were long, narrow, and pointed, and at so vast a distance from the black oaken floor as to be altogether inaccessible from within. Feeble gleams of encrimsoned light made their way through the trellised panes,**

and served to render sufficiently distinct the more promi-
nent objects around; the eye, however, struggled in vain to
reach the remoter angles of the chamber, or the recesses
of the vaulted and fretted ceiling. Dark draperies hung
upon the walls. The general furniture was profuse, comfort-
less, antique, and tattered. Many books and musical instruments lay scattered about, but failed to give any vitality
to the scene. I felt that I breathed an atmosphere of sorrow.
An air of stern, deep, and irredeemable gloom hung over
and pervaded all.

The narrator speaks of the mood of sorrow and fear and the atmosphere of gloom evoked by the room. What specific details of
the setting are most instrumental in creating this mood and atmosphere?

What particular words carry the strongest associative meanings?
Do sound and rhythm play a part in the creation of mood and atmosphere? Read the selection again, out loud, to help you answer
this.

In the story, of course, Poe uses all aspects of setting to create
a mood of fear and an atmosphere of melancholy and doom. The
landscape through which the narrator rides, the exterior and interior of the house, the storm outside, even the appearance of
Roderick Usher himself all contribute significantly to the effect the
story creates.

In "Rip Van Winkle," Irving uses setting to create an entirely different mood and atmosphere. Here are the opening paragraphs:

Whoever has made a voyage up the Hudson must remember the Kaatskill Mountains. They are a dismembered
branch of the great Appalachian family, and are seen away
to the west of the river, swelling up to a noble height, and
lording it over the surrounding country. Every change of
season, every change of weather, indeed, every hour of the
day produces some change in the magical hues and
shapes of these mountains; and they are regarded by all
the good wives, far and near, as perfect barometers. When
the weather is fair and settled, they are clothed in blue and
purple, and print their bold outlines on the clear evening
sky; but sometimes, when the rest of the landscape is
cloudless, they will gather a hood of gray vapors about
their summits, which, in the last rays of the setting sun,
will glow and light up like a crown of glory.

**At the foot of these fairy mountains, the voyager may have descried the light smoke curling up from a village, whose shingle roofs gleam among the trees just where the blue tints of the upland melt away into the fresh green of the nearer landscape. It is a little village of great antiquity, having been founded by some of the Dutch colonists in the early times of the province, just about the beginning of the government of the good Peter Stuyvesant (may he rest in peace!) and there were some of the houses of the original settlers standing within a few years, built of small yellow bricks brought from Holland, having latticed windows and gable fronts, surmounted with weathercocks.**

What mood does this setting evoke in the reader? What specific details develop it?

What atmosphere is created by the author's treatment of the mountains and village? What specific details contribute to the atmosphere? Why do you think Irving uses the words *"magical"* and *"fairy"* in describing the mountains?

Does the author's sentence structure and choice of words play a part in the creation of mood and atmosphere? If so, how?

Does the fact that the little villlage is "of great antiquity" have any significance?

In what respects is the setting appropriate to the story the author tells? What does it contribute to the story as a whole?

## Illuminating Character

A third use that you may make of setting is to illuminate or reveal character. For example, the physical details of the house a person lives in, the clothes a person wears, the possessions that a person values all reveal something about the kind of person he or she is. A person's reactions to a work of art, a landscape, seasons of the year, or times of the day can also be revealing.

Go back to *"The Flight of the Snowbird."* The setting is a rural scene, a farmhouse, a barn, a pasture, and a frozen pond. The story opens in the pale winter light of the early dusk of a wintry day. The setting, first of all, provides a stage for the action. But it also presents a beautiful pastoral scene and a season of the year with which many people have strong associations. Finally, it serves to illuminate the character of Benjy.

Read the first four paragraphs again. What is Benjy's reaction to the scene which he views from the window? Does this say anything about his character?

After Benjy leaves the house, slamming the door in anger, how does he react to the winter moonlight, the falling snow, and the gleaming pond? How is this reaction conveyed to the reader? Again, what does it tell us about the boy?

The conflict between Benjy and his sister is resolved at the end of the story. The relationship between the boy and the setting has revealed aspects of his character to us. Does this in any way prepare us for what happens? If so, how?

Look at the way another author uses setting in relation to character. Here's a passage from *Another Country,* by James Baldwin.

**Besides Vivaldo's phonograph, there wasn't much else in his apartment. There was a homemade lamp, brick-supported bookshelves, records, a sagging bed, the sprung easy chair, and the straight-backed chair. There was a high stool before Vivaldo's worktable on which Vivaldo teetered now, his coarse, curly black hair hanging forward, his eyes somber, and his mouth turned down. The table held his pencils, papers, his typewriter, and the telephone. In a small alcove was the kitchen in which the overhead light was burning. The sink was full of dirty dishes, topped by a jaggedly empty and open tin can. A paper sack of garbage leaned against one of the kitchen table's uncertain legs.**

In addition to providing a specific background, the details of the room also tell us something about Vivaldo himself. What details are most significant and what do they reveal to you?

Here's one more example. The following passage is from Henry James' *Washington Square:*

**She lived in a neat little house of red brick, which had been freshly painted, with the edges of the bricks very sharply marked out in white. . . There were green shutters upon the windows without slats, but pierced with little holes, arranged in groups; and before the house was a diminutive "yard," ornamented with a bush of mysterious character, and surrounded by a low wooden paling, painted in the same green as the shutters. The place looked like a magnified baby-house, and might have been taken down from a shelf in a toy-shop. Doctor Sloper, when he went to call,**

**said to himself, as he glanced at the objects I have enumerated, that Mrs. Montgomery was evidently a thrifty and self-respecting little person—the modest proportions of her dwelling seemed to indicate that she was of small stature—who took a virtuous satisfaction in keeping herself tidy... She received him in a little parlor, which was precisely the parlor he had expected: a small unspeckled bower, ornamented with a desultory foliage of tissue-paper, and with clusters of glass drops, amidst which—to carry out the analogy—the temperature of the leafy season was maintained by means of a cast-iron stove, emitting a dry blue flame, and smelling strongly of varnish.**

Dr. Sloper draws some conclusions about Mrs. Montgomery, whom he has never met, on the basis of her house. Which specific details of the setting support his conclusion that she was "thrifty" and "self-respecting"? Which support his conclusion that she is "tidy"?

What analogy does Dr. Sloper use to describe the little parlor? The setting reveals a number of things about Mrs. Montgomery. What does Dr. Sloper's reaction to it reveal about himself?

## Setting as Antagonist

A fourth way you might use setting is to establish it as the force with which your central character, the protagonist, is in conflict. One of the best illustrations of this is the way in which Thomas Hardy uses Egdon Heath in *Return of the Native*. The Heath is the principal force, or antagonist, with which Clym Yeobright is in conflict. In the beginning of the novel, Clym, the "Native," has returned to the Heath hoping to change its inhabitants through education. The vast, brooding, and timeless Heath, supremely indifferent to, if not actually hostile towards humans, is established as the force which shapes the destiny of Clym and of all the major characters. Hardy devotes the novel's first chapter, called *"A Face on Which Time Makes but Little Impression,"* to a description of the Heath. Here are some examples:

**The face of the heath by its mere complexion added half an hour to evening; it could in like manner retard the dawn, sadden noon, anticipate the frowning of storms scarcely generated, and intensify the opacity of a moonless midnight to a cause of shaking and dread.**

The place became full of a watchful intentness now; for when other things sank brooding to sleep the heath appeared slowly to awake and listen. Every night its Titanic form seemed to await something; but it had waited thus, unmoved, during so many centuries, through the crises of so many things, that it could only be imagined to await one last crisis—the final overthrow.

The untameable, Ishmaelitish thing that Egdon now was it always had been. Civilization was its enemy. . .

To recline on a stump of thorn in the central valley of Egdon, between afternoon and night, as now, where the eye could reach nothing of the world outside the summits and shoulders of heathland which filled the whole circumference of its glance, and to know that everything around and underneath had been from prehistoric times as unaltered as the stars overhead, gave ballast to the mind adrift on change. . .

As with some persons who have long lived apart, solitude seemed to look out of its countenance. It had a lonely face, suggesting tragical possibilities.

What is the dominant impression concerning the Heath which Hardy seeks to convey? What details develop this impression?

The opening chapter presents the Heath at twilight in the month of November. Is the season and time of day significant?

Point out instances where Hardy personifies the Heath (i.e., treats the Heath as if it were a person). What purpose does the personification serve?

The author uses the terms *"Titanic"* and *"Ishmaelitish"* to describe the Heath. Do you know the origin of the terms? If not, find out what they mean. Then think about why Hardy uses them as allusions to apply to the Heath.

What details clearly establish the Heath as the adversary of people? What functions does the setting have other than to act as adversary, or antagonist, in the conflict?

Here's another illustration of the use of setting as the antagonist. This conflict is in Jack London's story, *"To Build a Fire."* Here, as in *The Return of the Native,* an element of the setting is the force against which the central character, or protagonist, must struggle. It is this conflict between character and setting that forms the plot of the story. Here is a passage from the opening of the story:

The Yukon lay a mile wide and hidden under three feet of ice. On top of this ice were as many feet of snow. It was all pure white, rolling in gentle undulations where the ice-jams of the freeze-up had formed. North and south, as far as his eye could see, it was unbroken white, save for a dark hair-line that curved and twisted from around the spruce-covered island to the south, and that curved and twisted away into the north, where it disappeared behind another spruce-covered island. This dark hair-line was the trail—the main trail—that led south five hundred miles to the Chilcoot Pass, Dyea, and salt water; and that led north seventy miles to Dawson, and still on to the north a thousand miles to Nulato, and finally to St. Michael on Bering Sea, a thousand miles and half a thousand more.

But all this—the mysterious, far-reaching hair-line trail, the absence of sun from the sky, the tremendous cold, and the strangeness and weirdness of it all—made no impression on the man.

What particular aspects of setting does this passage present? How are the details organized?

Without reading anything else, can you figure out what particular element of setting will prove to be crucial in the conflict?

Although these illustrations have presented man in conflict with elemental forces of nature, other aspects of setting can be used with equal effectiveness. In Shirley Jackson's "*The Lottery,*" it is the civic ritual of the lottery that forms the basis for the conflict. Stephen Crane's *The Red Badge of Courage* depicts what happens to a young man under the conditions of war. Gordon Parks' *The Learning Tree* is the story of Newt's struggle against the social and economic prejudices of Cherokee Flats.

## Christmas Trees and Wedding Rings

Of course, you know what Christmas trees and wedding rings are. One is an evergreen tree decorated with ornaments and lights. The other is a ring widely used in the marriage ceremony. Is that all they mean? Probably not, for the Christmas tree has become a symbol of Christmas itself and the wedding ring a symbol of marriage itself. A symbol is something which has its own objective reality and yet stands for or means something else. A symbol can be an object, like the tree or the ring. It can be a person like a policeman who stands for law and order. It can be an action like

removing your hat, which is a sign of respect. A literary symbol is an object, person, or action in a story which has a literal meaning and yet stands for or represents other things as well.

A final way, then, that you may use setting is to employ a specific aspect of it in a symbolic way. In your use of literary symbols, however, you must be careful. The temptation of many beginning writers is to see symbols everywhere and to overuse them. In most stories details of setting operate almost entirely on the literal level. There are no simple formulas for the creation and the use of symbols. You should read widely and carefully enough to develop a sense of how experienced writers use symbols. In experimenting with symbolism in your own writing, keep in mind that the context of your story should establish that a detail is to be taken in a symbolic way and also make clear the meaning that the detail has within the story itself.

In the second paragraph of *"The Flight of the Snowbird,"* the author describes the bird as the boy sees it for the first time. What specific details of the bird does the boy notice? What is the dominant impression created by the bird? What details support this?

In the fourth paragraph, the boy's mother calls him and the bird flies away. Is there any difference between this impression of the bird and the boy's first impression? Why does he continue to watch it until it disappears?

Why does the author introduce the bird at this particular point in the story? Is there any suggestion that the bird, in the opening of the story, represents anything other than itself? Do you think it might be a symbol? Why or why not?

In paragraph thirty-one, the boy sees the bird again. Why is the bird introduced again at this precise point in the action? Do you think it is mere coincidence? Why or why not? If not, what purposes, in relation to the story as a whole, do you feel it serves?

Have you decided yet whether the bird is a symbol? Does it represent something in addition to itself? If so, what clues do the story and the title of the story provide about its meaning?

In *"The Fall of the House of Usher,"* Poe uses the physical house as a symbol of the family, or house, of Usher. As the narrator draws near the house, he notices its *"vacant and eyelike windows"* and its *"excessive antiquity."* Coming even closer he observes:

**Perhaps the eye of a scrutinizing observer might have discovered a barely perceptible fissure, which, extending from the roof of the building in front, made its way down the wall in a zigzag direction, until it became lost in the sullen waters of the tarn.**

Are the physical details, *"the vacant and eyelike windows,"* the *"excessive antiquity,"* and the *"barely perceptible fissure,"* enough basis for considering the house to be a symbol of the family itself? Why or why not?

Can you point out ways in which the house operates as a symbol throughout the entire context of the story?

We have presented five ways to use the elements of setting in writing a short story. Although we have described each way separately, it is common for a writer to use setting in several different ways in the same story. For example, the setting in *"The Flight of the Snowbird"* sets the stage for the action, creates a mood and atmosphere, illuminates the character of the boy, and provides a symbol that contributes to the meaning of the story.

You'll notice as you read the work of experienced writers that the nature and amount of physical detail used to develop the setting will vary according to its use and relative importance to the story. In Hemingway's *"The Killers,"* for example, setting is developed only minimally since it has no other function than to set the stage for the action.

On the other hand, in *"The Flight of the Snowbird"* and in *"The Fall of the House of Usher,"* it is more fully developed since in each story it plays an important part.

Much of your success in creating settings will depend on how well you develop your own powers of observation and upon how sensitive you become to the world around you. Filling your journal with "sounds, sights, smells, tastes, and textures of people, landscapes, events large and small" will help. Finally, it will depend upon the degree to which you have mastered the resources of language, its words, structures, sounds, and rhythms.

# Things to Do

Go back to your rewrite of the Parable of the Good Samaritan. Sketch out the details of place, time, and human environment that you would use if you were to develop it into a short story. Make this part of your journal.

Create a one-paragraph setting that will evoke any one of the following moods or atmosphere.

**fear**
**mystery**
**tranquility**
**melancholy**
**warmth**
**hostility**

Now go back to the list and do another one.

Write a one-paragraph setting of a room or of the exterior of a house that will reveal one or more of the following character traits:

**carelessness**
**thrift**
**meticulousness**
**poor taste**
**good taste**

Go back to the list of events in Chapter 5 concerned with Alan's running away from home. Select a conflict between Alan and one of the elements of setting indicated in the events. Outline the details you would include in a short story.

By this time your own short story should have a firm story line, a point of view and voice. Now consider in detail the elements of a setting that would work best and the ways in which you would make use of these details in your story. Jot down some notes and share them with your teacher or your friends.

# Chapter 8

## Creating Characters and Dialogue

It takes all kinds of people to make a world. And each person is unique. Even in your little part of the universe, there are more people than you could ever get to know during one lifetime. Even fewer are those that you could get to know well. How, then, does a writer create character? Upon what resources does a writer draw? Perhaps you have some character sketches in your journal. But even if you draw upon your journal entries and transcribe them literally from life to fiction, you would soon run out of these resources, so, what can a writer do?

Is a character in fiction simply a transcription, or copy, of someone the author knows in real life? Is the author merely a camera? The world of fiction is a make-believe world created by the writer, and the characters in it are make-believe characters. Although the world of fiction is a make-believe world, it is one which attempts to create an illusion of reality, to represent life.

If the characters are make-believe, not photographs but creations, out of what do you, as author, create them? Sue, Pete, Annie, and Tom are all different, but human nature itself has common elements—love and hate, laughter and tears. You get to know human nature by getting to know yourself and those close to you and by reading about and viewing human nature as presented in the work of experienced writers. Notice what makes people different by observing and recording actions, mannerisms, appearances, and conversations. This chapter will show you what kinds of characters an author can create, how to reveal character to the reader, and how to give characters speech through dialogue.

## Shapes and Changes

Some characters are flat and others are round. These terms don't refer to their physical shape, but to the complexity of development in the work. A flat character, sometimes called a type or caricature, is one constructed around no more than one or two ideas or qualities. For example, the protagonist in Jack London's *"To Build a Fire"* is a flat character, and the author tells us what his character is like at the beginning of the story:

**He was a newcomer in the land, a *chechaquo,* and this was his first winter. The trouble with him was that he was without imagination. He was quick and alert in the things of life, but only in the things, and not in the significances.**

What is the single idea or quality around which London has constructed his character?

Try to read the entire story if you haven't read it before. How does this single quality of the protagonist function?

A round character, on the other hand, is one which is more fully developed. A round character has all of the complexity of human nature, touching life not at one point but at many points. Mark Twain's *Huckleberry Finn* is an example of a round character. Because of its limited scope, the short story seldom lends itself to the development of fully rounded characters.

Characters may be classified as *static* or *dynamic*, depending on whether or not they change as a result of the actions developed in the plot. Go back to *"The Flight of the Snowbird."* Does the character of Benjy change as a result of what happens? Would you call him a dynamic character? Since the character of the protagonist in Jack London's story does not change, he would be a static character.

Flat or round, static or dynamic, your choice of what kind of character to create will depend upon the nature of your plot. Minor characters in a story are almost always flat and static simply because they are minor. The complexity and development of major characters will depend on what you do with the plot. Flat or round, static or dynamic, your characters must have a life of their own within the limits of your story. The rest of this chapter will deal with four ways of presenting character.

## Straight Out

One way to present characters is for you as author to tell straight out what a character is like. This can be done most effectively when you are using the omniscient point of view. For example, Jack London, in the passage previously quoted from *"To Build a Fire,"* tells us directly what his character is like. In Conrad's *"Youth,"* the narrator, Marlow, tells us about Captain Beard:

**He was sixty if a day; a little man, with a broad, not very straight back, with bowed shoulders and one leg more bandy than the other, he had that queer twisted-about appearance you see so often in men who work in the fields. He had a nut-cracker face—chin and nose trying to come together over a sunken mouth—and it was framed in iron-gray fluffy hair, that looked like a chin strap of cotton-wool sprinkled with coal dust. And he had blue eyes in that old face of his, which were amazingly like a boy's, with that candid expression some quite common men preserve to the end of their days by a rare internal gift of simplicity of heart and rectitude of soul.**

Conrad describes the physical appearance of the Captain so that the reader can just about see him. Do these same details reveal anything of the Captain's character?

What phrase in the description establishes the major idea or quality around which this character is constructed?

This technique of direct exposition of character is both clear and economical; however, it can never be used as the sole method of presenting character. There must be action, for without action there is no story.

## Actions Speak Louder

Action is a second way to present character. What the character does can tell a lot. In *"The Flight of the Snowbird,"* what purpose do the boy's actions serve in paragraphs five and six? Is there any significance, in paragraph seventeen, to his tipping the lawn chairs over? Note his actions in paragraph twenty-two. What do they tell us about Benjy? In the long last paragraph, what actions convey Benjy's change in attitude toward his sister?

Since Sheryl is unable to communicate verbally, her actions are extremely important in presenting her character. Go through the story and single out those actions which seem most important in revealing to the reader what Sheryl is like.

In presenting character through action, you must be careful that what the character does fits with his or her nature as you have developed it. If there is any discrepancy between what a character is and what he or she does, it should be used consciously by the author for ironic purposes. This is a difficult technique for a beginning writer.

## The Talk of the Town

In literature, as in life, people like to talk about other people. A third way of presenting a character is through what other characters say or think about the person.

In *"The Flight of the Snowbird,"* for example, much of what we know about Sheryl is conveyed through what other characters say and think about her. Look closely at paragraphs 13, 15, 23, 25, 27, 28. Could this information about Sheryl have been communicated in any other way? Is there more than one point of view expressed? Would you have written these paragraphs the same way?

Using what other people say can be an effective way of presenting information and insights about a character, particularly when your story is being told from other points of view than the omniscient and first person. You may also present conflicting viewpoints, but you must be careful that such conflicting views illuminate rather than obscure your character.

## Saying and Thinking

A final way you may present a character is by what the character says or thinks. For example, one of the most revealing insights into the character of Sydney Carton in Dickens' *A Tale of Two*

*Cities* is contained in the character's own words at the end of the novel:

**It is a far, far better thing that I do, than I have ever done; it is a far, far better rest that I go to, than I have ever known.**

Coming as it does immediately before Carton's execution on the guillotine, the statement serves as an unusually dramatic climax to the development of his character. What structural pattern does Dickens use to gain emphasis? Does this pattern also create a rhythm which is appropriate?

If your story is being presented from the omniscient or the third person limited point of view, you may present a character by what he or she thinks. This means that you are representing, without comment by yourself as author, the impact of actions or emotions upon the inner self of the character. For example, here is part of the opening paragraph of Conrad Aiken's *"Silent Snow, Secret Snow":*

**Just why it should have happened, or why it should have happened just when it did, he could not, of course, possibly have said; nor perhaps could it even have occurred to him to ask. The thing was above all a secret, something to be preciously concealed from Mother and Father; and to that very fact it owed an enormous part of its deliciousness. It was like a peculiarly beautiful trinket to be carried unmentioned in one's trouser-pocket—a rare stamp, an old coin, a few tiny gold links found trodden out of shape on the path in the park, a pebble of carnelian, a sea shell distinguishable from all others by an unusual spot or stripe— and, as if it were any one of these, he carried around with him everywhere a warm and persistent and increasingly beautiful sense of possession—it was also a sense of protection. It was as if, in some delightful way, his secret gave him a fortress, a wall behind which he could retreat into heavenly seclusion. This was almost the first thing he had noticed about it—apart from the oddness of the thing itself—and it was this that now again, for the fiftieth time, occurred to him, as he sat in the little schoolroom.**

This technique of representing the interior self of a character as though the reader were overhearing the stream of thought and feeling flowing through the character's mind is called the interior monologue.

Although at this point we do not know what the secret is that Paul is thinking about, we do get his reactions to it. Note the numerous figures of speech used to convey his reactions. Do any of them have anything in common?

The passage presents directly the thoughts and feelings of the little boy, and it reveals a number of things about him. But since it reveals them indirectly without comment or interpretation by the author, you must arrive at these things through inference. What kind of little boy is Paul? Does his extensive use of imagery and figurative language provide a clue?

What is Paul's relationship with his mother and father? For what does he seem to be desperately searching? Is there any suggestion of a conflict?

In what way is the voice and rhythm of the passage appropriate to the character and situation?

The interior monologue can at times be used as a flashback, which interrupts the action of the story to present a character's thoughts or memories concerning his past. In Hemingway's *"The Snows of Kilimanjaro,"* Harry, the protagonist, is dying and in several flashbacks remembers aspects of his past. Here is a part of one flashback:

**No, he had never written about Paris. Not the Paris that he cared about. But what about the rest that he had never written?**

**What about the ranch and the silvered gray of the sage brush, the quick, clear water in the irrigation ditches, and the heavy green of the alfalfa. The trail went up into the hills and the cattle in the summer were shy as deer. The bawling and the steady noise and slow moving mass raising a dust as you brought them down in the fall. And behind the mountains, the clear sharpness of the peak in the evening light and, riding down along the trail in the moonlight, bright across the valley. Now he remembered coming down through the timber in the dark holding the horse's tail when you could not see and all the stories that he meant to write.**

What does this reveal concerning the kind of person Harry was in his younger days? Do his thoughts and feelings suggest that he might have become a successful writer?

A character's past experience may have significance at the time the story is being told. Is there any hint in this excerpt as to why Hemingway uses the flashback? In what way might it illuminate Harry's character at the present time?

Here again are the four ways you, as an author, can present a character.

1. **Tell straight out what he or she is like.**
2. **Tell about the character through his or her actions.**
3. **Tell what others think about the character.**
4. **Reveal the character by what the character says and thinks.**

Most writers use all of these methods. Be especially careful to avoid overuse of the first method.

## Gray Ghosts and Real People

Your characters must be consistent, motivated, and lifelike. This is true no matter what combination of methods you use to reveal them.

First, they must be consistent in their behavior, in what they do and how they speak. Try to have your characters clearly in mind before you begin to write your story. Be able to see them and hear them speak, and know how they think. Their behavior shouldn't change as the story progresses unless there is good reason for the change. For example, at the end of *"The Flight of the Snow-bird"* there is a sudden change in Benjy's attitude toward his sister. Is sufficient reason provided for this change?

Second, your characters must be clearly motivated in whatever they do. For example, do you understand why Benjy hates his sister so intensely? Do you know why he decides to save her life? At the end of *A Tale of Two Cities,* is it logical that Sydney Carton should give his life for that of his friend? In *"To Build a Fire"* does the death of the protagonist follow logically from his character as described by the author at the beginning of the story?

Finally, your characters must be plausible. Have you ever read stories or seen films in which the characters appeared to be either all good or all bad? Can you believe characters like that? Are there really heroes without weakness and villains without virtue? At the beginning of *"The Flight of the Snowbird,"* Benjy's ruling passion is his hatred for his sister. Are any good aspects of his character revealed at the same time? A character is rarely all bad or all good. On the other hand, you should not present characters with impossible combinations of virtue and vice. Even though they are make-believe, your characters should be created in such a way that they appear to be real people.

## Talking Pictures

When films first came out with sound tracks, they were called *"talking pictures."* An effective way for you to create characters who are real people is to give them the gift of speech. But in making your characters talk, you must be careful that what they say and how they say it is consistent with their education, social position, special interests, and geographical location. For example, Huckleberry Finn is an uneducated boy who lives on the Mississippi River in Hannibal, Missouri, and who resists any efforts to be civilized. Here is how he talks:

**"Watchman your grandmother," I says; "there ain't nothing to watch but the texas and the pilot-house; and do you reckon anybody's going to resk his life for a texas and a pilot-house such a night as this, when it's likely to break up wash off down the river any minute?"**

In what specific ways is this the speech of an uneducated boy? How does the language reflect the part of the country where Huck lives?

Huck's special interests focus on the river. What details of his conversation reflect this?

Here's a completely different character speaking. This is the voice of Sherlock Holmes. Read his words and try to picture what he is like:

The presence of the gypsies, and the use of the word 'band,' which was used by the poor girl, no doubt to explain the appearance which she had caught a hurried glimpse of by the light of her match, were sufficient to put me upon an entirely wrong scent. I can only claim the merit that I instantly reconsidered my position when, however, it became clear to me that whatever danger threatened an occupant of the room could not come either from the window or the door.

Keep in mind that Sherlock Holmes is a well educated, well disciplined English gentleman and that he is a trained researcher and investigator. What characteristics of his speech reveal his education and discipline? What qualities are revealed that have made Holmes famous throughout the world as an investigator or detective?

## Give and Take

In addition to making sure that your characters speak in ways that make sense for them, try to make sure that they do not overdo making speeches. If dialogue is to further the action of your story, it must be a give and take between your characters, an interplay of personalities rather than a series of set speeches.

One of the most difficult aspects of writing dialogue is to handle it in such a way that different characters do not sound alike. In the following scene from John Steinbeck's "The Chrysanthemums," Elisa, a well-to-do rancher's wife, is talking to an itinerant tinker who has lost his way:

"I'm off my general road, ma'am," he said. "Does this dirt road cut over across the river to the Los Angeles highway?"

Elisa stood up and shoved the thick scissors in her apron pocket. "Well, yes, it does, but it winds around and then fords the river. I don't think your team could pull through the sand."

He replied with some asperity, "It might surprise you what them beasts can pull through."

"When they get started?" she asked.

He smiled for a second. "Yes. When they get started."

"Well," said Elisa, "I think you'll save time if you go back to the Salinas road and pick up the highway there."

He drew a big finger down the chicken wire and made it sing. "I ain't in any hurry, ma'am. I go from Seattle to San Diego and back every year. Takes all my time. About six months each way. I aim to follow nice weather."

Look carefully at the diction of both speakers and note the differences. How do you account for them? What is their effect?

Look carefully at the sentence structure of both speakers. Read the dialogue aloud. Is there difference in the rhythm? How is it created?

When you write dialogue for your characters, be sure that each one speaks in a way that makes sense.

How can you develop your skill in writing dialogue? First, continue to observe people and listen to them talk. Notice the differences in diction and sentence structure that distinguish speakers. Pay careful attention to dialogue in your reading where you can see how experienced writers work. Work at increasing the range and flexibility of your own vocabulary and knowledge of sentence structure. Practice creating dialogue for a variety of characters in a variety of situations.

# Things to Do

Write a brief character sketch in which you tell straight out what the character is like. Make sure that physical details of appearance and inner qualities of the character work together to create a unified impression. You may use a character in your short story or one from your journal. If you do not plan to use this sketch in your story, put it in your journal in final form.

Now develop an incident that will show a single aspect of the character sketched in the first activity. This need not be lengthy, but it should clearly reveal your character through action. If you are not going to use this material in your short story, enter it in your journal.

Now create a brief scene in which two people are talking about this same character you have already portrayed directly and through action. In this scene you may develop factual information about your character or you may wish to combine this with opinions of the speakers concerning the character. Use the scene in your story if you can. If not, make it part of your journal.

Write a brief interior monologue in which you reveal something about this same character. Have the character recall past experience or reproduce thoughts and feelings that are flowing through his or her consciousness at the present time. If you wish, you may combine this with the action in the incident you developed earlier. If you do, make sure that the interruption of the action by the monologue makes sense. Once again, save this for your story or make it an entry in your journal.

Write a brief scene in which your character is engaged in conversation with another person. Try to differentiate between the two by varying the diction and sentence structure. Read the dialogue aloud and listen to each voice. Make sure there is some interplay rather than set speeches by each. Try the dialogue on your friends to see if they can distinguish one speaker from another.

By now, you should probably be writing your short story. If you aren't, you should have accumulated the materials in your journal—story line, character sketches, settings—you should have made some firm decisions about voice and point of view. In short, you should start writing your story, if you haven't already.

## Putting It All Together

At this point, you may have the impression that you write a story by developing a plot, deciding upon voice and point of view, creating settings, and then adding the characters and dialogue, one step at a time. Of course, you know that this is not true. It's not that simple or organized. The set of skills having to do with plot construction, voice and point of view, and with creating setting, characters, and dialogue should be helpful. However, it still may not happen easily.

If you have been working on elements of your own story in the recent exercises, you are well on your way. But wouldn't it be nice if you could just put it all together with tape? Of course, it's not that simple. Even experienced authors have to work hard at it. The first draft may need to be revised a number of times. But keep at it. See what works best for you.

When you finish this story, how do you get started on your next story and the next one? How do you start? Each author uses the ways that work best for him or herself, though in the writing of the story each must work with the same basic techniques you have been using.

Where can you begin?

Read, observe, and listen! Actually, you have been doing these things since you started keeping a journal. That will continue to be a reliable source of ideas because it's handy and because its entries reflect your own experience. When looking for an idea for a story, stick to subjects, people, and places you know. And finally, as Henry James said, "Try to be one of the people on whom nothing is lost!"

*There should never be an incident, a scene, a comment in your story that doesn't move it toward its climax.*

Judson Philips

# Chapter 9

## Writing a Play:

### The Elements of Stagecraft
### The Structure of a Play

Stories are written to be read. Plays are written to be seen. Look again at the two sequences of illustrations. They show you how your relationship to the readers of the short story you just wrote differs from a playwright's relationship to the viewers of a play he or she has written.

The words of your short story were read directly by your readers. You chose the point of view from which to address them. If they liked the story they could reread all or part of it at their leisure. A play is different from a short story. Like a story, a play uses words and sentences. The written words, however, are not directly consumed by a reader as are the words in a short story. A play is meant to be performed. The playwright uses objective point of view, because the writing must first be interpreted by a director, then performed by actors. Each participant will add something to the work. Ultimately, what the audience will see will be strongly influenced by the talents and skills of a great many people other than you, the author. When you write, you must think of the next person in line who will read your words. For fiction, that person is the reader. For drama, you must write for the people who will be staging your play. You will always, of course, keep in mind the ultimate effect you intend your play to have.

You don't need to know much about printing or publishing in order to write a short story. However, it helps to know something about stages and stagecraft when you try to write a play. Such knowledge allows you to communicate clearly to the director, actors, and technicians who will be using your script. It will also determine to some extent the kind of play you write and the techniques you can and cannot use to accomplish your purposes.

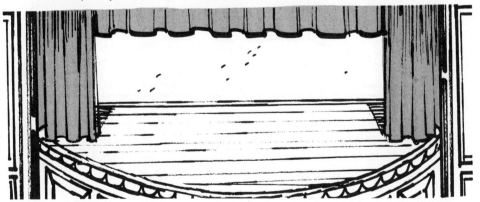

## Looking in through a Window

This picture shows you the kind of stage you probably should write for. It's called a proscenium stage. It's shaped like an open-sided box so that the audience views the action as through a giant window or picture called the proscenium arch. There are other types of stages, but the proscenium is the most popular and probably best serves the needs of a beginning writer.

Look at this diagram of a proscenium stage as viewed from above. It shows you the major acting areas. It may come in handy when you try to write directions for your performers. Note that areas are labeled from the point of view of the performers on the stage, not the point of view of the people in the audience.

| | | |
|---|---|---|
| **up<br>right** | **up·<br>center** | **up<br>left** |
| **right<br>center** | **center** | **left<br>center** |
| **down<br>right** | **down<br>center** | **down<br>left** |

## Paper Moons and Canvas Walls

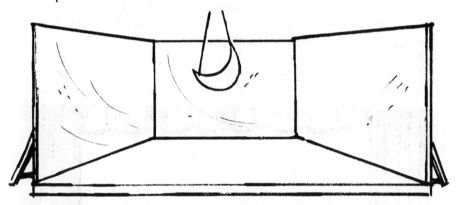

Some plays can be produced on a bare stage, but most would be enhanced by scenery. One of the advantages of a proscenium stage is its flexibility in providing for scenery, which makes up the three sides of the box into which the audience looks.

As the author of a play, you need not know how to construct scenery or build a set, but you must have a set in mind as you write. If not, you will be unable to give consistent stage directions to the actors, and you might forget that the view of the audience is limited to one side. Also, if you don't visualize the set beforehand, you might end up with inconvenient or even silly situations for floor plans or placement of furniture in interior sets.

Generally it's best not to clutter or complicate a set unnecessarily. Everything on stage should serve a purpose. Remember that the audience should be able to figure out the design, function, and meaning of the set without labels over doors or footnotes in the program.

## Props, but not to Lean On

In addition to scenery, most plays use stage properties, or props as they are called. This term can apply to all objects other than scenery used by performers. It includes furniture. Most often it refers to hand props, the portable objects found on the set or carried on by the actor. Objects may be able to tell your audience more than words can. This is important, because you, the author, cannot speak directly to the audience. Sometimes props simply add to the reality of the set. Or, they may permit an actor to perform "business," activities more elaborate than gestures, which help reveal the nature of a character. Occasionally, props can even serve as a major symbol for the theme of a play. It is the job of the author to determine which props are essential to the story. Props having a more important function than decorating the set should be designated by you in your script. However, don't ask the impossible or require too many.

## Illuminating Sights and Sounds

Imagine a play brilliantly written, sensitively directed and acted—on a dark stage in pantomime. Nothing. The effect would add up to nothing without sight and sound, the two final elements of stagecraft that the author of a play should consider.

Naturally, some aspects of light and sound can be delegated to the backstage technicians, the director, and the actors. It's hardly necessary for the script to tell the director to provide light so the audience can see. However, special lighting effects can be written into your script. Special sound effects or music can also be specified in your script if you wish. As you write your play and visualize it in final staged form, think about what special lighting or sound effects could enhance its performance and then write directions for these effects along with your script.

# Conventions

All literature makes use of conventions in the sense that authors tend to observe and readers accept certain practices of form, style, and subject matter. For example, sonnets have fourteen lines, Alexander Pope wrote in heroic couplets, and Anglo-Saxon verse relied upon an alliterative beat. Drama, as a genre of literature, has its own conventions. These allow the author and performers to depart from reality in certain traditional ways, without having to explain their actions. The audience is willing to accept these practices as part of play production. Some conventions apply mainly to the performances of the actors. The audience readily accepts the overall convention of these performers being imitators or impersonators, along with such specific departures from reality as actors speaking with abnormal volume, wearing costumes, and even talking to themselves. What would you think if you saw someone doing any of these things outside the theater?

Staging also involves conventions. One major convention which the audience accepts is that the stage represents an actual geographical setting. The audience also accepts such specific distortions as viewing the action from a fourth wall point of view, and being placed in separate, lower, darkened position. The use of a curtain signals members of the audience to turn off acceptance of this artificial world and return to their own reality.

Studying the conventions of the theater can help you use them to your advantage. Beginning writers should abide by these conventions and try to work with them. As you become more experienced in writing plays, you may want to create some special effects by breaking ·one or more of the conventions. Think about some of the possibilities.

What effects would be created, for instance, if you broke the impersonator convention by having a member of the audience come up on the stage? What might be the results if you had actors speak in a normal conversational volume while acting?

Since most modern plays don't tend to use soliloquies or choruses, what accepted conventions might you use to reveal inner thoughts or give comments about the development of the play?

Think about breaking the convention of audience placement by seating the audience on stage, or by staging an entire play in a public street or park. What advantages might this have? What disadvantages?

Can you name some plays which do not use the convention of an opening or closing curtain? What effects does this technique achieve?

It's best to begin with the accepted conventions when you begin writing your first play. However, some of today's conventions were yesterday's experiments. Think about special effects. Perhaps some day you too could make a contribution to drama.

## Things to Do

Take a trip to a nearby stage, in your school if there is one, or wherever else you can. Learn as much about its operation as possible. You might even be able to help in the production of a play. This would be a good way to learn how plays are really produced.

Read as many plays as possible, to see how the author gives directions for production. Note the stage directions for set, props, lights, sound, and actor movement. Here are a few suggestions of plays that might interest you. Your teacher can provide a longer list.

**Riders to the Sea** *by John Synge*
**Our Town** *by Thornton Wilder*
**A Raisin in the Sun** *by Lorraine Hansberry*
**The Zoo Story** *by Edward Albee*
**West Side Story** *by Arthur Laurent*

**Long Day's Journey into Night** *by Eugene O'Neill*
**Pygmalion** *by George Bernard Shaw*
**Miss Julie** *by August Strindberg*
**Macbeth** *by William Shakespeare*

See as many different plays as you can. Try to read each of the scripts at least once beforehand. Take special note of any breaks in convention employed within these plays and the effects these breaks attempt to achieve.

## Playwright or Playwrite? Which is Right?

These three pictures form a riddle of sorts. Can you tell what they have in common? Here's a hint: Their common feature concerns the way in which each one was made or constructed. Give up? The answer is that each of these items is constructed by a person known as a wright—a shipwright, a wheelwright, and a playwright. You can write a play, but in doing so you become a playwright.

Wright means *"one who constructs."* A playwright constructs a play. You can construct a play much as you did your short story, building incident upon incident. Each scene or incident contributes to the development of the plot. In drama, the plot is usually called the action. Scenes differ from incidents in that they are usually more clearly defined or set off. In full length plays scenes are often indicated by pulling the main curtain. Scenes may be set off by the entrances or exits of characters or by obvious shifts in the action. Scenes are often marked by major moves across stage or by relatively long periods of silence.

In general, the action of a play is developed in the same manner as a fictional plot. In a short story, the beginning establishes the setting, presents the characters, and provides an initial incident. In a play, the opening scene is called the *exposition*. Its purpose is to explain whatever the members of the audience cannot see for themselves. In this sense, the scene serves as an initial incident. It reveals something about the characters, it shows their motives for being at that particular place and for acting in a certain way, and it sets up or suggests the forthcoming conflict. Succeeding scenes, like incidents in a story, provide the rising action or *complication*.

The major characters interact as the conflict is developed. Gradually the action reaches a *crisis,* a structural turning point. Then comes the *falling action,* which often includes a relief scene to break the tension or show the passage of time. Finally, the ending, or *resolution,* must tie everything together and point toward the theme of the play. Read a play or two and see how the scenes follow the pattern just outlined.

## Things to Do

Read a one-act play and identify the conflict developed. Write a short paragraph explaining the conflict.

Based upon your determination of the conflict in a play you've read, write a scenario of the play. (A scenario is a scene by scene outline.) Concentrate on the development of the conflict.

If you have an idea for a scenario of your own, write it as you just wrote the scenario for a play that you read. In some cases a single statement about the purpose of each scene will be enough. For some scenes you will need to make a statement for each segment within the scene. Remember to keep it short. A scenario is an outline, not a retelling of the action.

## Meaning

Like a short story, a play has a theme, something the author is trying to show us about human nature or life in general. Like a good fiction writer, a playwright does not reveal the theme directly. Only in the poorest plays will a character speak a line that completely sums up everything the play is trying to say.

From your study and analysis of *"The Flight of the Snowbird,"* you know that one approach to theme can be through the title of a work. Think about the play you are planning to write. Are you ready yet to create a title? Do you want your title to suggest the theme? Why or why not?

Another approach to the theme of a play can be taken by considering its setting: the place, time, and human environment. Place is the obvious ingredient of setting. Setting includes the time in which the events occurred, as well as where. Some playwrights purposely state that the work takes place in "the present." They then avoid any specific references to song titles, dance fads, current events, or anything that might date their play. The human environment is also an important part of setting. The social, moral, religious, and/or economic standing of the characters in a play may contribute significantly to setting. Think about these factors in relation to a play you have recently read. Which of them, if any, were a vital part of setting?

## Structure's the Key

Title and setting have to be considered in determining the theme of a play, but so must structure. In fact, a number of critics today feel that structure, or how the plot or action is revealed, is the most reliable and significant means of determining the meaning of a work. If such a judgement is valid, it must certainly apply to one-act plays. The writers of one-act plays have very little time or space in which to reveal the action. Everything must count.

In determining how structure can reveal the theme of a work, you must first ask yourself the questions, "What has the author shown us?" and "What has the author not shown us?" Try this with one of the one-act plays you have read.

Structuring a creative work is really the art of selection, an art which separates fiction and drama from real life. To write, authors must use lifelike events. They must select the *"right"* ones and place them in the *"right"* order—not too vague, not too contrived, saying only what needs to be said.

*I have a tendency, after a play of mine is produced, to look back on it disparagingly, seeing only its faults (before production, I see only its virtues).*

William Inge

# Things to Do

If you haven't yet written a scenario for a play of your own, do so now. Remember a scenario is a scene by scene outline of a play.

It is not necessary to state the theme of your play in writing, but discuss your scenario with others. Take notes on their ideas as to its meaning or their suggestions for its development. Then change or add to your scenario anything you think will improve its structure.

*Take some wood and canvas and nails and things. Build yourself a theatre, a stage, light it, learn about it. When you've done that you will probably know how to write a play.*

Eugene O'Neill

*A convention is an agreed-upon falsehood, a permitted lie.*

Thornton Wilder

*It is, perhaps more than anything else, the arrest of time which has taken place in a completed work of art that gives to certain plays their feeling of depth and significance.*

Tennessee Williams

*Our Town is not offered as a picture of life in a New Hampshire village; . . . It is an attempt to find a value above all price for the smallest events in our daily life.*

Thornton Wilder

# Chapter 10

## Visualizing and Creating Setting

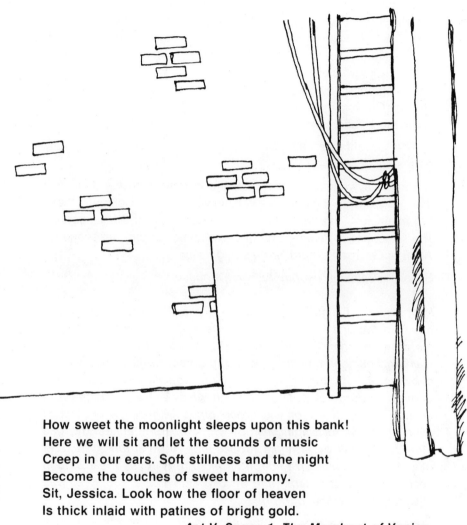

How sweet the moonlight sleeps upon this bank!
Here we will sit and let the sounds of music
Creep in our ears. Soft stillness and the night
Become the touches of sweet harmony.
Sit, Jessica. Look how the floor of heaven
Is thick inlaid with patines of bright gold.

**Act V, Scene 1, The Merchant of Venice**

That's one way to create setting. In these few lines, Lorenzo in *The Merchant of Venice* turns a bare stage into a setting filled with moonlight, stillness, and stars. Would it have been more effective if the words had been replaced by blue-gelled floodlights and a false ceiling speckled with 40-watt bulbs? Is what you see necessarily more real than what you can imagine? Every play must occur somewhere and every playwright has to create that setting. How it's done can vary greatly.

# The Where, When, and Who of Setting

A play, like a story, must occur in a prescribed place, a geographical location with a physical environment. In a story you must tell about the country, the town, the street, or the room, and describe the sounds, smells, weather, or objects that are necessary to the scene. The play's audience, like the reader of a story, also needs to know these things. To accomplish this, you may use a bare stage and have the characters describe the scene for the audience. Or, you may call for a realistic set where everything but taste, touch, and smell is shown or visually suggested.

What advantages can you see to using a stylized set or totally bare stage for a play?

Some playwrights are very detailed in describing the setting of their plays, while others give very few directions. Compare these two examples. The first sets the scene for Act V of Shakespeare's *The Merchant of Venice*. The other describes in part the scene for Act II of George Bernard Shaw's *Pygmalion*.

Scene 1. *Balmont. Avenue to Portia's house.*

*Next day at 11 a.m. Higgins' laboratory in Wimpole Street. It is a room on the first floor, looking on the street, and was meant for the drawing room. The double doors are in the middle of the back wall; and persons entering find in the corner to their right two file cabinets at right angles to one another against the walls. In this corner stands a flat writing table, on which are a phonograph, a laryngoscope, a row of tiny organ pipes with bellows, a set of lamp chimneys for singing flames with burners attached to a gas plug in the wall by an india rubber tube, several tuning forks of different sizes, a life-size image of half a human head, showing in section the vocal organs, and a box containing a supply of wax cylinders for the phonograph.*

*Further down the room, on the same side, is a fireplace, with a comfortable leather-covered easy chair at the side of the hearth nearest the door, and a coal scuttle. There is a clock on the mantelpiece. Between the fireplace and the phonograph table is a stand for newspapers.*

What advantages would there be in providing all the details of setting in your script? What disadvantages?

Time too is a part of setting. It may refer to a historical period, a season of the year, or a particular time of day. If any of these

elements is important, it must be designed in the script. This places an additional responsibility on the director who wishes to stage the play authentically. For example, a play set in the Victorian age would not appropriately use furniture of the late twentieth century. Think about the time of day your play will use. Will this require directions from you for an interior set? For an exterior set?

The last element of setting is the human environment, and here too, the author can either be explicit or allow the director and actors to interpret the characters as they choose based upon the action of the play. In *The Merchant of Venice,* Shakespeare introduces Jessica in Act II, scene III with a simple *"Enter Jessica. . . ."* Shaw, however, in *Pygmalion* describes Liza, the flower girl, in Act I, scene I, like this.

*She is not at all an attractive person. She is perhaps eighteen, perhaps twenty, hardly older. She wears a little sailor hat of black straw that has long been exposed to the dust and soot of London and has seldom if ever been brushed. Her hair needs washing rather badly: its mousy color can hardly be natural. She wears a shoddy black coat that reaches nearly to her knees and is shaped to her waist. She has a brown skirt with a coarse apron. Her boots are much the worse for wear. She is no doubt as clean as she can afford to be; but compared to the ladies she is very dirty. Her features are no worse than theirs; but their condition leaves something to be desired; and she needs the services of a dentist.*

What are the advantages of giving a detailed description of a character's social standing or particular views on social subjects? What are the disadvantages?

Can you think of some of the characteristics a director would have to decide upon for the nature of Jessica in *The Merchant of Venice*?

Based on Shaw's description of Liza, what conclusions could an actor or audience draw about her social and economic position? What could be said about her attitude toward her own position as a street vendor?

## The Why of Setting

In *Our Town,* by Thornton Wilder, the Stage Manager opens the play by walking onto a bare stage. After setting out tables and chairs, he checks the time, casts a disapproving eye at latecomers, then introduces the play by naming title and author, director and technical staff, and identifying the town (Grovers Corners, N.H.) and a particular date in history (May 7, 1901). For the exact words of this introduction, read the material in italics at the beginning of *Our Town.*

This introduction to Thornton Wilder's play gives us a setting: a place, a time, and a human environment—all the physical elements just discussed. All settings must reveal these elements to a greater or lesser extent. The primary purpose of setting is to provide a location for the action of the play. But beyond these physical requirements lie a number of other purposes which a setting can accomplish. The setting can also create atmosphere. Think of some plays you have read. Has the atmosphere of the setting contributed to the theme?

Closely associated with atmosphere is the ability of setting to illuminate character. The setting provides a place for characters to perform. It must also be appropriate to the type of people being portrayed, and ideally, give the audience some clues as to their nature.

Think about setting in some of the plays you have read. How does it help tell you about character?

In helping to reveal character, setting must of necessity be closely related to the conflict of a play. In some plays, however, setting can serve the same purpose that it does in certain works of fiction. Setting can be the antagonist, the force against which the characters are in conflict. For example, the use of setting as antagonist can clearly be seen in naturalistic plays like Elmer Rice's *Street Scene* or Sidney Kingsley's *Dead End*. In both of these, people struggle against a physical environment clearly depicted by the setting.

A final purpose of setting allows the stage to serve both the specific and the general at the same time. This occurs when a setting reveals a symbolic purpose. A symbol, as you know, is something concrete which takes on or portrays a universal meaning.

For an example of symbolic use of setting, look again at the opening to *Our Town*. Wilder could have chosen to use a fully realistic setting to depict the town of Grover's Corners. Instead he used a bare stage, sparsely set by the Stage Manager in full view of the audience. What symbolic theme might the bare stage help create in relation to Wilder's view of the lives of the people who live in Grover's Corners?

*My greatest trouble is getting the curtain up and down.*

T. S. Eliot

At times even a realistic set can be symbolic. Jean-Paul Sartre's one-act play, *No Exit,* depicts an elaborately decorated drawing room, with no mirrors, no windows, and a door locked from the outside. Within the play, we are told that the setting represents Hell. How would the physical aspects just mentioned help to symbolize the nature of eternal punishment?

In creating a setting for your own play keep some guidelines in mind. Provide enough physical setting so that the place, time, and human environment are amply and appropriately suggested, but do not go into extreme detail in your stage directions. Let the director make some decisions too. On the other hand, try to create a setting that serves more than the fundamental purpose of providing a physical acting area. Describe the set so that the scenery, props, and action suggest an atmosphere that is appropriate to the theme and will help reveal the nature of the characters within the play. But here too, don't go too far. Creating a setting which either is meant to serve as an antagonist or has symbolic value is difficult. You may want to experiment with these ideas in your later writing, but your early effort should probably not be that complicated. For a start, keep your setting simple. Show the people in your audience what they need to know. Lines like "How sweet the moonlight sleeps upon this bank!" worked for Shakespeare, but they probably wouldn't work as well for you.

# Things to Do

Review some of the plays you've read or seen and study their settings. Choose one of them that you think gives a good example of setting. Write a paragraph describing the purposes which the setting fulfills.

Using your written scenario and your ideas on a theme for an original one-act play, write the opening stage directions which will establish the place, time, and human environment for your play.

Discuss your setting with others in terms of its varied purposes. Think about it carefully again. Revise it if necessary.

*A work of art is never finished, it's abandoned.*

André Gide

*Once you're on the stage you have no time, because the stage is to experience—you follow?—the stage is to experience.*

Sidney Poitier

*Good actors are good because of the things they can tell us without talking.*

Sir Cedric Hardwicke

*Characterization in a play is like a blank check which the dramatist accords to the actor for him to fill in.*

Thornton Wilder

*. . . actions, not words, are the true criterion . . .*

George Washington

# Chapter 11

## Visualizing and Creating Character

**Ned.** That'll do, Bill! *(Holds hand in front of Bill's pistol)* You mean well, but I can fight my own battles.

**Bill.** *(Comes down R.C.)* Not with a cockle-doodle-do like Blackman Redburn! He don't fight fair an' square!

*Black'n.* I'll fight it with you fair and square whenever yore a-mind to.

*Ned.* Reckon here and now will fill the bill. Pick up your poppinjay.

*Black'n. (Picks up gun)* Fifteen paces with pistols? The winner takes the gal? *(Looks at Lily)*

*Ned.* Good enough. But since there's ladies present we'll do it outside. Bill, go pace off the ground. You be my second!

*Bill.* Keeno. *(Runs out shouting)* Pilgrims! Here's a duel! . . .

    *(Black'n exits; Ned starts to follow)*

*Lily. (Calls)* Wait, sir! Tell me what are you about to do?

*Ned. (Goes to her)* Nothing much. Take care of that cad who insulted you.

*Lily.* You would fight a duel because of me? Oh, sir, I beg of you, peril not your life!

*Ned.* Nonsense. There is no danger. I can split a playin' card at fifteen paces. Go over there and watch from the window. *(Points to window, then turns to go.)*

*Lily.* Oh, sir, do you not know that I have eyes which see not?

*Ned. (Turns, looks at her)* Blind? Why you poor little hummingbird. Now my ire is up! I'll blast that Blackman Redburn from the face of the earth! *(Exits C drawing two six-guns)*

Don't laugh! Those lines are from a real play, and one that accomplishes what it sets out to do. The play is Tom Taggart's *Deadwood Dick*, the ultimate parody of a western and a melodrama to end all melodramas. The characters are typed, good versus bad; they're transparent, and predictable. Despite this, the natures of the characters are revealed in much the same manner as those in most other plays. This chapter will show you some common types of characters and techniques you can use to reveal the roles they are to play.

## Typed and Other Types

Who was the villain in the *Deadwood Dick* excerpt? Who was the hero?

If you were producing the play what traditional costume and makeup would you choose for the villain? What for the hero?

These were easy questions to answer, weren't they? The characters in *Deadwood Dick* are typed or stock characters. Stock characters are predictable. Everyone—writers, actors, and audiences—can predict their natures, their looks, and even their actions. Part of the fun of seeing a melodrama lies in this easy game of recognition, since all the characters are of this stock variety.

But stock characters can be used effectively in nonmelodramatic plays as well, as long as they are not major characters and they serve a useful purpose in the play. Stock characters can people your stage and act as foils, but unless it's melodrama you're after, you can't build a play around them.

For building a play there are five principal types of characters—round or flat, dynamic or static, and catalysts. *Round* characters are fully developed and show a number of major characteristics. *Flat* characters exhibit only one or two major characteristics. Fully developed or "round" characters are most frequently found in long works of fiction or drama. Most short stories or one-act plays use less developed or "flat" characters for both major and minor roles, simply because there is insufficient time or space to develop greater complexity.

Besides being classified as flat or round, characters can also be designated by what happens to them during the action of the play. If major characters change appreciably during a play, they are *dynamic* characters. Little or no change categorizes them as *static*.

The fifth type of character is one, other than a protagonist, who precipitates change in others, but does not change himself. Through an analogy to chemistry, such a character is called a *catalyst*. Many full-length and one-act plays do use catalysts. In *Macbeth* the three witches serve this function. In *A Man for All Seasons,* Rich is the catalyst. In both, the catalysts are less developed than the characters and do not change. However, they are crucial to the development of the action and the nature of the protagonists.

***Some mystery should be left in the revelation of character in a play, just as a great deal of mystery is always left in the revelation of character in life, even in one's own character to himself.***

Tennessee Williams (stage directions for *Cat on a Hot Tin Roof*)

# Things to Do

Review some of the plays you've read or seen, and try to classify the major and minor characters of each as flat, round, static, dynamic, or catalytic.

Do some of the categories overlap? Why?

Why is it difficult to classify some characters precisely?

## Show and Tell

**Back to *Deadwood:***
*Ned. (Enters C. . . . Takes solid stance, hands on gun butts.*
*Ned is everything a hero should be—big, handsome, noble.)*

**Ned. That'll do Bill! . . . You mean well, but I can fight my own battles.**
**Bill. Not with a cockle-doodle-do like Blackman Redburn! He don't fight fair an' square!**

Two basic methods to reveal character—show them and tell them. Who does the showing and who does the telling? To answer these questions in detail and apply the answers to your own writing, you'll have to understand four basic techniques for revealing character. Some parallel the techniques used in fiction; others do not.

One technique is exemplified by Taggart's description of Ned: "*everything a hero should be—big, handsome, noble.*" This is direct exposition by the author. The character is described in straightforward terms. The description may be rather terse as it is here since Taggart is dealing with a stock character, or it may be very detailed as was Shaw's description of Liza on page 123.

Besides describing them in parenthetical italics, the author must also name the characters, and this too can help reveal their natures. In older fiction and drama, writers frequently used tag names or titles which actually described or suggested a flat character's dominant characteristic. Dickens' use of *Gradgrind* for a teacher or Thackeray's use of *Deuceace* for a gambler are examples.

Would you consider any of the names used in *Deadwood* tag names?

Modern playwrights except melodrama writers don't tend to use such an obvious technique as tag names. Nevertheless, most authors choose names for their characters with some care.

The second technique for revealing character is exemplified by Bill's description of Blackman Redburn in *Deadwood:* *"He don't fight fair an' square."* This is an indirect approach. In this case the author tells about a character through another character. In direct exposition the author speaks directly to an actor without telling the audience in words. The audience only has the actor's interpretation of the exposition to determine what the author intended. In indirect description, however, the audience does hear the words, and therefore must take into account who is speaking the lines. The audience must determine whether one character's statement about another is valid, and if not, what motive the speaker might have for misrepresenting the other character.

In relation to Bill's lines in *Deadwood,* the audience would most likely accept his description of Blackman Redburn as dramatic truth. The play deals in absolutes and no one would expect such a heinous villain to *"fight fair an' square."*

Ancient Greek and some modern plays use a chorus to describe characters and interpret actions. Why might their descriptions be less questionable than those given by a regular member of the cast?

Other plays, like *Our Town* or *A Man for All Seasons,* use a narrator to give description. Can you always assume that this person is really the author speaking directly to the audience?

A third technique for revealing character, also indirect, can be shown by Blackman Redburn's reply to Bill's accusation of his never fighting "fair an' square." Blackman replied: *"I'll fight it with you fair and square whenever yore a-mind to."* The villain lies— we'd hardly expect him to do otherwise—yet his line still exemplifies how an author can reveal character by having the character describe himself.

In Shakespearian times, playwrights used the convention of soliloquy to accomplish this kind of self-revelation. But now the soliloquy is no longer an accepted convention. So playwrights must resort to more realistic methods such as having a character talk about him or herself in conversation.

The fourth technique for revealing character involves showing rather than telling. Here, as in fiction, the author can reveal the nature of characters by having them act or perform. But a great many differences exist between the way characters perform in fiction and the way they act on stage. In fiction the author has total control. Nothing is revealed unless it's written. In drama, the playwright has much less control. Actors can never stop acting on stage. They must perform constantly and every move counts. Fortunately, the total responsibility for directing this action does not fall upon you, the playwright. Some things can be left to the discretion of the director and actors. A playwright must set forth in the script whatever is crucial to the revelation of character or the development of the action.

What kind of things should you include in your description when you write a play? Generally, you should specify any body position or activity which will communicate an essential, nonverbal message. It may be a specific posture, gesture, business, movement, or some combination of these to indicate a physical or mental state—age, deafness, tiredness, anxiety. Specific placement of a character in relation to the rest of the cast can suggest either congeniality or alienation. Some, but never all characters can be set apart or accentuated by being given certain mannerisms which help reveal or support their roles. And in some cases, it is even necessary for the playwright to designate the use of specific costumes, makeup, or props to help reveal some important aspect of a particular character.

In writing a play, no one method of revealing character should be used to the exclusion of all others. Direct exposition normally is used whenever a character is introduced for the first time. Generally from then on, the author uses a variety of indirect approaches, revealing each character gradually as the action develops.

As you write your one-act play, ask yourself these questions about the way your characters are developed.

*Motivation*—Is it clear to the audience why each character performs or speaks at the time and in the manner you've indicated?

*Consistency*—Are all of the statements, actions, and motivations of a character appropriate to the one or two dominant characteristics you have emphasized in his or her individual nature?

*Plausibility*—Do the natures of the characters present a realistic balance between the universal and the unique so that the roles being portrayed are human and credible?

In some situations, the playwright can rely upon the performers' abilities to improvise. The actors can determine for themselves what actions and lines would be appropriate to fill in. In other cases, if the playwright wants to insure that some lines will actually be spoken, it might be necessary to suggest in the stage directions that the actors ad lib, or create spontaneous lines, with a few examples being suggested by the author.

Balance in dialogue also means that there must be give and take among performers. Long speeches are often difficult for an audience to grasp and place an added burden on the performers as well. During long speeches both giver and recipient must fill in with appropriate but nondistracting movements while speaking or listening.

Here's another point. Write your dialogue so that each major character is distinctly set off or differentiated from the rest of the people in the play. Though the parts in a play will often reflect a certain commonality of background—social, regional, occupational—each performer should speak in a different "voice," one that reflects a particular nature.

Be careful. In writing dialogue that is meant to reflect the individual characteristics, make sure that you use language that accurately depicts these characteristics. In other words, if you want to reveal a particular character as a member of a certain group, you must know exactly how the people in that group normally speak. However, in writing exact dialogue, don't go too far. You can and should suggest certain qualities through diction, usage, and sometimes sentence structure, but let the director or actor decide how a particular dialect is to sound. For example, look at these lines from Lorraine Hansberry's *A Raisin in the Sun*.

**Mama.** *(To Beneatha)* **Why you got to flit so from one thing to another, baby?**
**Beneatha.** *(Sharply)* **I just want to learn to play the guitar. Is there anything wrong with that?**
**Mama.** **Ain't nobody trying to stop you. I just wonders sometimes why you has to flit so from one thing to another all the time. You ain't never done nothing with all that camera equipment you brought home—**
**Beneatha.** **I don't flit! I—I experiment with different forms of expression—**

Beneatha, the daughter, is a college student, whereas Mama has not had a great amount of education. How do the diction and usage employed by each of them reflect this difference?

But notice that the exact way the words should sound is left to the performers on stage. However, later in the play, Walter, the son, speaks this line as he parodies with great bitterness the dialect of a southern slave.

**Yassssuh! Great White Father, just gi' ussen de money, fo' God's sake, and we's ain't gwine come out deh and dirty up yo' white folks neighborhood. . .**

This use of sight dialect is effective. It serves a purpose and helps to reveal the speaker's motives. But unless you're trying to create some type of special effect such as this, don't try to duplicate exact speech sounds when writing dialogue.

Try to write dialogue that is both pleasing to read and natural to speak. This isn't always an easy thing to do. It helps to avoid extremes. On one hand you are writing literature. This means your statements must be concise and meaningful. On the other hand, you're also writing speeches, which means your statements must be natural. However, they cannot reflect all of the hesitations, repetitions, and looseness of everyday conversation. These contrast-

135

ing requirements will force you to compromise. You must write with both an eye and an ear for language. Read what you write both silently and aloud. Have others read your script to you, preferably having a different person reading each part. These techniques will help you revise your initial efforts. Gradually you will learn to write with the needs of both the critical audience and the performing actors in mind.

## Things to Do

By now you should have an outline or scenario for an original one-act play, along with an opening description of a setting. You may wish to revise your scenario now. If so, keep in mind what you've learned about character types and balance of presentation.

Write a character sketch for each speaking part in your play. Make sure the minor characters are revealed only to the extent that they relate directly to the major characters and the conflict being enacted by them. Also be sure that you limit the characteristics of the major characters so that they are not developed into "round" types. Your play won't be long enough for that. Whatever is revealed about them must relate directly to the conflict while still portraying them as believable people with whom the audience can empathize.

Next write the opening descriptions for each major character or group of characters. Write these in italics (or underline each word) and place them in parentheses in your script.

Now, write the first draft of your play. At this point, concentrate on dialogue. You can insert minor stage directions later. Use a variety of techniques to reveal each character. Based on the character sketches you wrote, write dialogue which will reveal the nature or voice of each role. Balance the speeches by creating interaction, and write the lines in meaningful prose which has a natural ring. That's all there is to it!

## Revising and Staging—Staging and Revising

**March 27, 1930**

**Read over first draft M.B.E.** [*Mourning Becomes Electra,* a **three-act play]—scrawny stuff but serves purpose as first draft—parts damned thrilling but lots more lousy—not enough meat. . .—reading this first draft I get feeling that more of my ideas was left out of play than there is in it!—In next version I must correct this at all costs—run the risk of going to other cluttered-up extreme—use every means to gain depth and scope—can always cut what is unnecessary afterwards.**

*Working notes and extracts from*
*a fragmentary work diary by*
*Eugene O'Neill.*

Did you receive some similar impressions from the appraisal of your first draft? One quality illustrated by O'Neill's notes is his amazing ability to evaluate and criticize his own writing. This skill is important for a playwright. Work on it. Let a first draft sit and ferment for awhile. Then approach it critically, rereading it several times, always (as much as possible) as if you had never seen the work before. For now, you have others—teacher and classmates—to help you evaluate your work. Later, you will have to rely more heavily on your own critical sense.

*. . . choose a subject that is within your powers, and ponder long what your shoulders can and cannot bear.*

Horace

*Could I put it more shortly? Have I said anything avoidably ugly?*

George Orwell

You should plan on rewriting your first draft at least once. Ask for help on any aspect that needs improving, but be especially conscious of the need to tighten up the development. Make sure every line accomplishes something in relation to character revelation or development of plot. And don't be in too much of a hurry to turn out a finished product. Notice what O'Neill says here.

**March 31, 1930**

**Start writing 2nd draft.**

**July 11, 1930**

**Finish 2nd draft—feel drained out—have been working morning, afternoon and night every day, without a single let-up—never worked so intensively over such a long period. . . —wish now I'd never attempted the damn' thing—bitten off more than can chew?—Too close to it to see anything but blur of words—discouraged reaction natural now.**

Discouragement is natural. But don't let it get to you. You can do it, with time and persistent effort and help. Remember the work you did reworking your short story?

Reworking a play involves an important extra step. Plays are meant to be performed, not just read, and staging your work is the best way to test its strength and weaknesses. Seeing is still believing.

How do you stage your work? Look for opportunities both in school and out. Wherever and whenever possible you should do it, and revise it as it's being performed. Perhaps you could even video tape the performance so you can make additional revisions as you and others view it and criticize it.

What judgments should you make in revising your play? Unfortunately there is no formula to follow. Certainly, you should listen to others and by all means go back and study what you've read here, wherever you detect a weakness in your writing. Here's some advice, again given by O'Neill in his notes, as he continues in his entry for July 11th.

**Too close to see anything but a blur of words—discouraged reaction natural now—after all, do know I was deeply moved by each play as I wrote it—that test has always proved valid heretofore—lay it aside now—we are off to Paris tomorrow—nice little vacation in dentist's chair scheduled! Best anodyne for pernicious brooding over one's inadequacies, that!—anything else seems like the best of all possible when your nerves are prancing to sweet and low down of a dental drill!**

*Revise!* **Then go get your teeth filled!**

*The writer creates, and as he does, he plays a role or assumes a voice . . .*

Robert M. Gorrell

*Begin at the beginning and go on till you reach the end: then stop.*

The King of Hearts

# Chapter 12

## Writing Poetry:

### Concentrating on Images Timing and Rhyming

Ponder for a moment the different ways you use language every day. You can and do send or receive messages all the time without consciously having to concentrate on the techniques of language that you are using. How, for instance, have you used language in the last hour or two? Have you told a joke, a secret to a friend, an anecdote in class, or your tale of woe about last night's homework?

You don't have to think about language in these ways, do you? The techniques are a natural part of you. In the last few hours you've used sound, imagery, narration, and even dramatic climax. And, you probably haven't thought about it at all. These techniques are natural—inherent in the use of language.

When you write creatively, you must use these techniques somewhat more consciously than when you engage in conversation. The creative writer employs techniques of language according to the conventions which form the literary genre being used. You've already worked with fiction in your short story and with drama in your one-act play. These next pages are designed to help you deal with the conventions of still another genre—poetry.

Begin with this poem by Robert Frost. Read it and see how it differs from the way the same thing might be said in a conversation.

## A Time to Talk

When a friend calls to me from the road
And slows his horse to a meaning walk,
I don't stand still and look around
On all the hills I haven't hoed,
And shout from where I am, "What is it?"
No, not as there is a time to talk.
I thrust my hoe in the mellow ground,
Blade-end up and five feet tall,
And plod: I go up to the stone wall
For a friendly visit.

*Robert Frost*
*(1874-1963)*

What does the poem say? Suppose you wanted to communicate its theme, or overall message, using a different genre of literature. How might you say the same thing in a short story? How might you relate the incident in the scene of a play?

## Haiku

To begin our work with writing poetry, we're going to start with an ancient poetic form that has its own specific set of conventions. Here are three examples of this form.

> **Neither earth nor sky;**
> **Nothing left, only the snow**
> **Falling fast oh fast.**
>
> *Hashin (19th century)*

> **As bell tones fade,**
> **blossom scents take up the ringing—**
> **evening shade!**
>
> *Basho (1644-1694)*

> **Fall moon arises**
> **Leaving nighttime laughter in**
> **the river ripples.**
>
> *Annie (20th century)*

The three poems you have just read are examples of haiku, a form of Japanese poetry with very set rules. Look back at the poems again and see what these rules are.

Count the syllables in each poem. How many are there? How are they arranged in each line? The traditional Japanese haiku employs seventeen syllables in three lines—five in the first, seven in the second, and five in the last. The second haiku you read, in which the lines have four, eight, and four syllables respectively, rather than the traditional five, seven, five, illustrates what often happens when Japanese is translated into English. In the translation it's often quite difficult to keep the precise arrangement of syllables. You, of course, should have no such difficulty, since you will be writing your haiku in English to begin with.

The haiku has rules about imagery as well as structure. Look at each of the poems again. Note that they contain images referring to nature and suggesting a season. Which of the seasons is suggested by each of the poems?

What are the major images in each of the poems? How do the images in a poem interact with each other or with what the poet is trying to say? Does the interaction of images suggest a parallel between a change in nature and a change in human life? Could you rephrase the suggested parallelism in prose?

The limited number of words and syllables permitted in haiku and certain other forms of Oriental verse results in concentrated and very intense images to carry meaning. These images can have connotations far beyond the simple words on the page. What a given poem means has far greater dimensions than the seventeen syllables.

Look at the Japanese brush painting on the next page. The lines suggest bigger visual forms. Like the brush lines in the painting, the images in a poem can suggest connotations far beyond what the eye can see or the ear can hear directly. With this in mind, go back to the three haiku and consider the images again.

## Things to Do

Now it's time to try writing haiku yourself. Remember the rules:

**17 syllables, arranged in three lines**

**5 syllables in the first line, 7 in the next, and 5 in the last**

**image referring to nature with suggestion of season of the year**

**possible parallelism between change in nature and change in human condition**

Try a few and see how they work. You might find it easier to write out your thoughts for a poem in prose first. Then you can work on condensing your words and images to fit the conventions of the haiku.

## Tanka

Another form of Japanese poetry that uses concentrated imagery is tanka. It is a very popular form of writing in Japan today.

Here is an example of tanka. Read it over once to get an overall impression. Then go back and see what inferences you can make about its structure.

Lying here alone,
So lost in thinking of you
I forgot to comb
My tangled tresses—oh for
Your hand caressing them smooth!

*Lady Izumi Shikibu*
*(tenth century)*

Fortunately, this translation duplicates the traditional Japanese structure. What is the pattern of syllables for each of the five lines? How many syllables are there in all?

Look at the syllable count for the first three lines again. Does the arrangement remind you of the haiku? It should. Historically, the haiku can be traced back to tanka. Take the first three lines of tanka in terms of structure, concentrate imagery to convey nature and hint of the season, and you will have a haiku.

# Things to Do

Try writing tanka. Keep in mind the rules of structure:

**31 syllables in all**
**5 lines, with syllable arrangement 5,7,5,7 and 7**

Unlike haiku, your imagery need not imply the season or nature (although it may, if you wish). Once again, you might find it helpful to write your thoughts in prose before structuring your tanka according to the rules.

Find a partner and together try writing tanka in the traditional Japanese manner. One person writes the first three lines and the other writes the last two. Originally, tanka was always composed in this manner. After you have composed your first tanka as a team, reverse roles and try another one. This will give each of you practice in composing both the beginning and end of the poem.

## Cinquain

The traditional Japanese tanka also influenced the development of cinquain, a type of American verse with conventions similar to the Oriental style. Here's an example of cinquain:

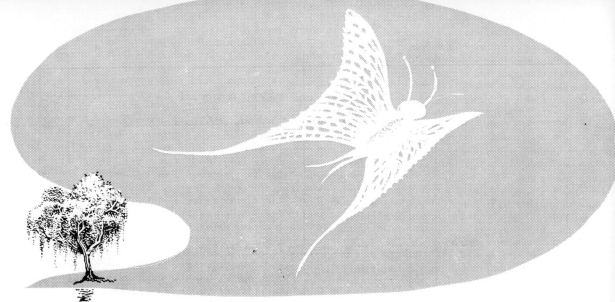

## Cinquain: A Warning

Just now,
Out of the strange
Still dusk . . . as strange, as still . . .
A white moth flew. Why am I grown
So cold?

Adelaide Crapsey
(1878-1914)

How many syllables are there in all? How many lines? What is the arrangement of the syllables?

Think for a moment about the 2,4,6,8,2 arrangement of syllables. Does this seem to result in a more climactic description than the two Japanese forms you have just worked with? Why, or why not?

## Things to Do

Now try writing your own poem according to the conventions of cinquain. Remember the rules:

**22 syllables in all**
**5 lines, with the syllables arranged 2,4,6,8,2**

The content and type of imagery you use in a cinquain is up to you. Once again, you might wish to put your thoughts in a prose statement before focusing on the structure of the poem.

# Concrete Poetry

Another form of poetry that uses very concentrated imagery is concrete poetry. Concrete poetry is constructed so that the verbal message and the visual form work together to communicate what the poet has in mind. One of the best known concrete poems is **Apfel,** *by Reinhard Döhl.* Here it is.

**PATTERN POEM WITH AN ELUSIVE INTRUDER**

ApfelApfelApfelApfel
ApfelApfelApfelApfelApfelA
ApfelApfelApfelApfelApfelApfe
ApfelApfelApfelApfelApfelApf
pfelApfelApfelApfelApfelApfel
ApfelApfelApfelApfelApfelApfe
pfelApfelApfelApfelApfelApfelA
ApfelApfelApfelApfelApfelApfe
ApfelApfelApfelApfelApfel
ApfelApfelApfelApfelApfelApf
ApfelApfelApfelWurmAp
ApfelApfelApfelApfel
ApfelApfelApfel
ApfelApfelA
ApfelApfel

*Reinhard Döhl ( b. 1934 )*

Sometimes the imagery is quite abstract, as in this poem.

## ARCHIVES

```
generation upon
generation upon
generation upon
generation upon
generation upon
generation upon
generation upon
generation upon
generation upon
generation upon
generation upon
generation upon
generation upon
generation upon
generation upon
generation upon
generation upon
generation upon
generation upon
g neration upon
g neration up n
g nerat on up n
g nerat  n up n
g nerat  n  p n
g  erat  n  p n
g  era   n  p n
g  era   n    n
g  er    n    n
g   r    n    n
g        n    n
g        n
g
```

Imagination and surprise are essential ingredients in concrete poetry. The visual image may be quite obvious, as in these two poems.

```
                      Dusk
                  Above the
              water hang the
                      loud
                      flies
                  Here
                  O so
                  gray
                  then
                  What            A pale signal will appear
                  When         Soon before its shadow fades
                  Where        Here in this pool of opened eye
                  In us     No Upon us As at the very edges
                 of where we take shape in the dark air
                   this object bares its image awakening
                     ripples of recognition that will
                       brush darkness up into light
       even after this bird this hour both drift by atop the perfect sad instant now
                       already passing out of sight
                       toward yet-untroubled reflection
                   this image bears its object darkening
                 into memorial shades Scattered bits of
                 light     No of water Or something across
                 water        Breaking up No Being regathered
                 soon          Yet by then a swan will have
                 gone             Yes out of mind into what
                  vast
                  pale
                  hush
                  of a
                  place        SWAN AND SHADOW
                  past
              sudden dark as
                 if a swan
                  sang                    John Hollander
```

Casting a long shadow

```
        Walking
         alone
          at
     night, often
     makes one
      stop and
     think about
       the day
     almost gone.
       and    with
       the    day
      ones    dreams.
       but    just
        as     there
       will    be
      other    days,
      there    will
        be     other
       dre     ams.
        i      hope
       all     my
     dreams    will
       not     pass
        as     easily
        as     the
       next    day.
```

                    -greg-

Here's one more concrete poem. Can you get its message?
Look very closely at the detail.

The title of this poem is *lilac*. Would you have guessed that?
Can you see why?

# Things to Do

Now try writing some concrete poetry of your own. If you have trouble getting started, try selecting the visual image first and then writing a message to go with it. If you're still stuck, here are some suggestions. Could you plan words to go with the shape of a chair? a telephone? an animal? a plant? Go to it!

## Timing and Rhyming

You've already tried your hand at writing a few poems—some, such as haiku, tanka and cinquain—according to some very precise rules of structure. Now it's time to talk about some of the other essential ingredients of poetic construction—rhythm and rhyme scheme.

The techniques of natural language that you've studied earlier in this book—techniques such as connotation, figures of speech, alliteration, onomotopoeia, or repetition—can be found in poetry as well as the prose selections you looked at earlier. Poetry is primarily an aural genre—that is, it is meant to be listened to, rather than simply read. Therefore, the sounds a poem uses are of utmost importance. Especially important in a poem is the use of patterned rhythm and patterned rhyme.

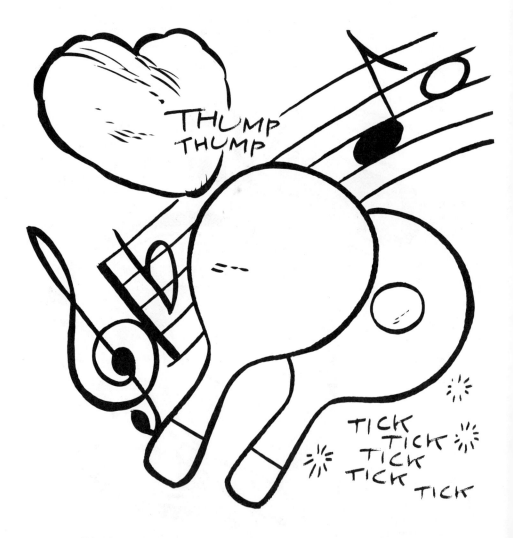

Rhythm is a natural part of life. The first sounds a person hears are the rhythmic heartbeats of the mother. From birth to death, rhythm is an essential ingredient of one's life.

Language, too, has rhythm. In English, every word of more than one syllable has a natural rhythm of accented and unaccented syllables. Accented syllables can be indicated with a mark like this ╱. Unaccented syllables are marked with ∪. Here are some examples. Say them out loud.

control

laughter

intertwine

yesterday

## Things to Do

Now look back at some of the haiku you read or wrote earlier in the chapter. Copy two or three of them onto a sheet of paper and mark the accented and unaccented syllables. Compare your work with that of your classmates.

## Verse

When accented syllables are arranged so that they seem to occur at equal intervals, the result is verse—metered or metrical language. Here are two lines of verse of a very well-known poem:

The time has come the walrus said

To speak of many things

Notice how the accents occur regularly.

*It is with words as with sunbeams—the more they are condensed, the deeper they burn.*

Robert Southey

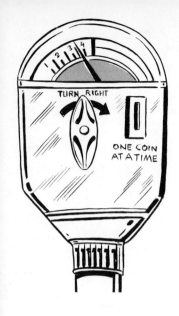

What does this picture have to do with poetry? Not much, really. It is, of course, a parking meter, and its main purpose here is to introduce the word *meter*. The word *meter* comes from Greek and means "measure." In poetry, there are two fundamental units of meter, or rhythmic measurement. The basic unit of meter is the foot. A foot consists of one accented and one or two unaccented syllables. Here are four varied foot patterns, along with the technical name for each one, and a word as an example.

ᵕ / Iambic    control

/ ᵕ Trochaic    laughter

ᵕ ᵕ / Anapestic   intertwine

/ ᵕ ᵕ Dactylic   yesterday

A word with two accented syllables results in a foot called Spondee.

nighttime

Words with no accented syllables give a Pyrrhic foot.

and the

The English language does not permit a spoken line to have all accented or all unaccented syllables, so that English poetry which uses meter must rely upon the first four metrical forms listed above, rather than on Spondee or Pyrrhic.

# Things to Do

Write a list of multisyllabic words. Pick words that you find interesting. Mark the syllables in each and see if you can label each according to its metrical form.

## Lines

The second unit of poetic measurement is the line. Each line has a number of feet, or repeated patterns. A line can have only one foot or as many as eight. Rarely does a line have more than eight feet. Here are the technical words that describe how many feet there are per line:

| | | | |
|---|---|---|---|
| 1 | Monometer | 5 | Pentameter |
| 2 | Dimeter | 6 | Hexameter |
| 3 | Trimeter | 7 | Heptameter |
| 4 | Tetrameter | 8 | Octameter |

# Things to Do

Experiment with lines of different lengths. Try writing some original verses using different numbers and kinds of feet. The lines may be serious or, if you prefer, nonsense. The purpose here is to play with meter so that you get practice with different rhythms.

Pick a poem that you like. Be sure that it's one in which rhythm seems to be an important factor. Mark the accented and unaccented syllables. Then count the feet per line. See if you can come up with the correct label for the poem's meter (e.g. iambic pentameter, anapestic tetrameter, etc.) Measuring poems in this way is called *scansion*.

## The Importance of Rhythm

Some poems have a meter or beat that is easily recognized. Others do not. Why do poems differ? Here are two poems by the same poet, Rudyard Kipling. One has a very pronounced, even exaggerated beat. The other has meter that is much more subtle. Read the two poems out loud several times and compare. How do the differences enhance the meaning?

# BOOTS

## INFANTRY COLUMNS

We're foot—slog—slog—slog—sloggin' over Africa—
Foot—foot—foot—foot—sloggin' over Africa—
(Boots—boots—boots—boots—movin' up an' down again!)
    There's no discharge in the war!

Seven—six—eleven—five—nine-an'-twenty mile to-day—
Four—eleven—seventeen—thirty-two the day before—
(Boots—boots—boots—boots—movin' up an' down again!)
    There's no discharge in the war!

Don't—don't—don't—don't—look at what's in front of you.
(Boots—boots—boots—boots—movin' up an' down again);
Men—men—men—men—men go mad with watchin' em,
    An' there's no discharge in the war!

Try—try—try—try—to think o' something different—
Oh—my—God—keep—me from goin' lunatic!
(Boots—boots—boots—boots—movin' up an' down again!)
    There's no discharge in the war!

Count—count—count—count—the bullets in the bandoliers.
If—your—eyes—drop—they will get atop o' you!
(Boots—boots—boots—boots—movin' up an' down again)—
    There's no discharge in the war!

We—can—stick—out—'unger, thirst, an' weariness,
But—not—not—not—not the chronic sight of 'em—
Boots—boots—boots—boots—movin' up an' down again,
    An' there's no discharge in the war!

'Tain't—so—bad—by—day because o' company,
But night—brings—long—strings—o' forty thousand million
Boots—boots—boots—boots—movin' up an' down again.
    There's no discharge in the war!

I—'ave—marched—six—weeks in 'Ell an' certify
It—is—not—fire—devils, dark, or anything,
But boots—boots—boots—boots—movin' up an' down again,
    An' there's no discharge in the war!

*Rudyard Kipling*

# IF—

If you can keep your head when all about you
   Are losing theirs and blaming it on you,
If you can trust yourself when all men doubt you,
   But make allowance for their doubting too;
If you can wait and not be tired by waiting,
   Or being lied about, don't deal in lies,
Or being hated, don't give way to hating,
   And yet don't look too good, nor talk too wise:

If you can dream—and not make dreams your master;
   If you can think—and not make thoughts your aim;
If you can meet with Triumph and Disaster
   And treat those two impostors just the same;
If you can bear to hear the truth you've spoken
   Twisted by knaves to make a trap for fools,
Or watch the things you gave your life to, broken,
   And stoop and build 'em up with worn-out tools:

If you can make one heap of all your winnings
   And risk it on one turn of pitch-and-toss,
And lose, and start again at your beginnings
   And never breathe a word about your loss;
If you can force your heart and nerve and sinew
   To serve your turn long after they are gone,
And so hold on when there is nothing in you
   Except the Will which says to them: "Hold on!"

If you can talk with crowds and keep your virtue,
   Or walk with Kings—nor lose the common touch,
If neither foes nor loving friends can hurt you,
   If all men count with you, but none too much;
If you can fill the unforgiving minute
   With sixty seconds' worth of distance run,
Yours is the Earth and everything that's in it,
   And—which is more—you'll be a Man, my son!

*Rudyard Kipling*

# Rhyming

Rhyme serves two basic purposes in poetry. Rhyming provides repetition of like sounds without repeating identical words. It provides a pattern for organizing lines of verse into poetic paragraphs, or stanzas. Not all poetry utilizes rhyme, but using rhyme can enable the poet to intensify the melodic quality of the verse and to strengthen the organizational pattern. Or, rhymes can simply make poetry more fun, as in the case of nursery rhymes or the nonsense verse of Ogden Nash or Dr. Seuss.

Contrast the qualities of repetition and rhyming in poetry to the same qualities in prose. In prose, the repetition of identical words can be effective to achieve emphasis, but rhyming is usually inappropriate and even distracting. Read this sentence out loud and see what rhyme can do to prose.

*"The police suspected that the man in the sedan was casing the local bank."*

The prose paragraph is not intended to be as highly structured a unit of organization as the stanza is in poetry.

English is often not an easy language to rhyme. There are two major types of rhyme patterns. One pattern has the like sounds occurring in only one accented syllable. Here are some examples:

**cry and why     divorce and enforce**
**house and mouse**

The second type of pattern has sounds that are alike occurring in two or more syllables. Here are some examples:

**Mertyl and turtle**
**spitefully and delightfully**

The most obvious and predictable use of these rhyming patterns is at the ends of lines. However, rhyme can also occur internally, within a line of poetry. Also, poetry frequently makes use of approximate rhymes, or sounds which almost make it as perfect rhymes, but not quite.

*All things are symbols.*

Henry W. Longfellow

Read this poem out loud. See if you can find the different rhyming techniques just discussed.

## *Song:* The Splendor Falls

The splendor falls on castle walls
    And snowy summits old in story:
The long light shakes across the lakes,
    And the wild cataract leaps in glory.
Blow, bugle, set the wild echoes flying,
Blow, bugle: answer, echoes, dying, dying, dying.

O, hark, O, hear! how thin and clear,
    And thinner, clearer, farther going!
O, sweet and far from cliff and scar
    The horns of Elfland faintly blowing!
Blow, let us hear the purple glens replying,
Blow, bugle: answer, echoes, dying, dying, dying.

O love, they die in yon rich sky,
    They faint on hill or field or river:
Our echoes roll from soul to soul,
    And grow for ever and for ever.
Blow, bugle, blow, set the wild echoes flying,
And answer, echoes, answer, dying, dying, dying.

                  *Alfred, Lord Tennyson (1809-1892)*

When end rhyme is used in a poem, the repeated patterns of final sounds usually determine the length of the stanzas. A quatrain has four lines, with alternate lines rhyming. A couplet has two lines of equal length with end rhymes. Sometimes quatrains and couplets combine to make a stanza. Look again at the poem by Tennyson. Note that each six line stanza is made up of a quatrain and a couplet.

**At its most effective a symbol is like a many-faceted jewel: it flashes different colors when turned in the light.**
                  Laurence Perrine

# Limericks

Limericks have been around for a long time. No one really knows where they came from or when they began. Limericks have certain rules for meter and rhyme scheme. They are fun to read and write, and they can give you practice in working with meter and rhyme. Here is a very well known limerick.

**There was an old man of Peru**
**Who dreamt he was eating his shoe**
**He awoke in the night**
**In a terrible fright**
**And found it was perfectly true!**

Here is a limerick that was written by Mary Mitchell, a high school student.

**There once was a young man named Todd,**
**Who was such a terrible clod,**
**He walked down the hall,**
**Ran into a wall,**
**And injured his poor little bod.**

Here is another well-known limerick:

**There was a young woman named Bright**
**Whose speed was much faster than light.**
**She set out one day**
**In a relative way**
**And returned on the previous night.**

If you study limericks carefully, you should find five anapestic lines. Lines one, two, and five are trimeter. Lines three and four are dimeter. The rhyming scheme is *aabba*. In other words, lines one, two, and five rhyme (a) and lines three and four (b) rhyme. Now here's another limerick. Think of the rules carefully and then read it out loud.

**A decrepit old gas man named Peter,**
**While hunting around for the meter,**
   **Touched a leak with his light**
   **He arose out of sight**
**And, as anyone can see by reading this, he**
   **also destroyed the meter.**

# Things to Do

Now try your hand at writing a limerick or two.

## Thinking About Meter and Rhyme

You have just studied some technical material about poetic construction. Does this mean that every time you sit down to write a poem you have to think out in advance all the technical attributes of your potential poem? Does a poet really sit down and say, *"Today I'm going to write three quatrains of dactylic tetrameter"*? Of course not! These little pieces of technical information are presented here to help you out if you need them. They are not meant to be an obstacle to writing poetry straight from your heart to the paper. Try putting your words down in writing. Then read them out loud. If they don't "work"—that is if the rhythm or rhyme doesn't sound quite right—then you may wish to analyze the technical aspects of your meter or rhyme according to the guidelines just outlined. But, if the poem sounds right the way it is, you need never go back and scan the lines.

# Things to Do

Try writing a poem. Any poem. Don't fret or worry about feet or rhyme schemes. Just write. Then, if you feel the need, you can study your lines and refine them.

# Chapter 13

## Telling A Poetic Tale

Throughout the ages poetry has served a great many purposes. In almost every culture, poetry was one of the earliest forms of personal or social expression. Among famous examples in history are the writings of Homer, the psalms of David, and the songs of Anglo-Saxon gleemen.

Poetry, like music, sometimes just seems to happen, spontaneously. For many centuries the great masses of people in Western civilization were illiterate and so they relied on oral literature. They sang and sang again their stories of love and death and humor and heroism. These tales were sung and passed on from generation to generation. Most of these tales took the form of ballads.

# Ballads

Here is an example of an early English ballad.

## Lord Randal

"O where hae ye been, Lord Randal, my son?
  O where hae ye been, my handsome young man?"
"I hae been to the wild wood: mother, make my bed soon,
  For I'm weary wi' hunting, and fain wald lie down."

"Where gat ye your dinner, Lord Randal, my son?
  Where gat ye your dinner, my handsome young man?"
"I din'd wi' my true-love: mother, make my bed soon,
  For I'm weary wi' hunting, and fain wald lie down."

"What became of your bloodhounds, Lord Randal, my son?
  What became of your bloodhounds, my handsome young man?"
"O they swell'd and they died: mother, make my bed soon,
  For I'm weary wi' hunting, and fain wald lie down."

"O I fear ye are poisoned, Lord Randal, my son!
  O I fear ye are poisoned, my handsome young man!"
"O yes! I am poison'd: mother, make my bed soon,
  For I'm sick at the heart, and fain wald lie down."

Generally speaking, English folk ballads used quatrain stanzas with an iambic tetrameter line. The rhyme scheme was usually *abcb* or, from time to time, *abab*. Look back at *"Lord Randal,"* and note its meter and its rhyme scheme.

Many ballads used a repeated question or a statement as a refrain. This served as a unifying element both for the theme and the music. It emphasized a major part of the poem for the listeners.

Ballads were oral and had to be memorized. Because of this, they usually focused on a single dramatic incident, but one that often implied a larger action or cause. The details of the event within a ballad's tale were vivid and presented directly with little or no character development, interpretation, or moralizing over virtue or vices.

Characters in ballads committed good deeds—acts of bravery, mercy, or love—and bad—thievery, murder, cruelty and the like. The ballad simply told the story.

There may be a number of printed versions of a given ballad. Here's one version of a very popular one. Nearly one hundred different verions of this ballad can be found in American folklore. The version given here is fairly close to the original Scottish story. A few words have been translated into contemporary English to make the ballad easier to read.

## Bonny Barbara Allan

It was in and about the Martinmas time,
   When the green leaves were a-falling,
That Sir John Graeme, in the West Country,
   Fell in love with Barbara Allan.

He sent his men down through the town
   To the place where she was dwelling:
"O haste and come to my master dear,
   If ye be Barbara Allan."

O slowly, slowly rose she up,
   To the place where he was lying,
And when she drew the curtain by,
   "Young man, I think you're dying."

"O it's I'm sick, and very, very sick,
   And it's a' for Barbara Allan:"
"O the better for me ye's never be,
   Though your heart's blood were spilling."

"Don't you mind, young man," said she,
   "When the red wine ye were fillin',
That ye made the healths gae round and round,
   And slighted Barbara Allan?"

He turned his face unto the wall,
   And death was with him dealing:
"Adieu, adieu, my dear friends all,
   And be kind to Barbara Allan."

And slowly, slowly raise she up,
  And slowly, slowly left him,
And, sighing, said she could not stay,
  Since death of life had reft him.

She had not game a mile but two,
  When she heard the dead-bell ringing,
And every stroke that the dead-bell gave,
  It cried, "Woe to Barbara Allan!"

"O mother, mother, make my bed!
  O make it saft and narrow!
Since my love died for me today,
  I'll die for him tomorrow."

They buried her in the old churchyard,
  And Sir John's grave was nigh her.
And from his heart great a red, red rose,
  And from her heart a brier.

They grew to the top o' the old church wall,
  Till they could grow no higher,
Until they tied a true love's knot—
  The red rose and the brier.


Try to find some American ballads. One well known blues ballad is *"Stagger Lee."* Perhaps you will even be able to locate a record of it. Another more recent ballad is *"Ode to Billy Jo."* It was a popular hit record. See what ballads you can locate either in song sheets or on records or tapes.

Ask yourself these questions as you read or listen to a ballad. What are the details of the event? Is there a refrain that keeps reinforcing or unifying the major point the ballad tells? Does the song tell us anything about the people other than what they did? What is the meter and rhyme scheme used? Is it consistent?

Try to locate both the song sheet and the record or tape for one ballad. Listen to it and then read it. Are the words most effective when read silently, read aloud, or sung? Why?

Here is a ballad. It was a popular hit in the winter of 1976-77 in many parts of the country. Gordon Lightfoot, the Canadian folksinger, wrote the words and music and recorded this ballad.

## The Wreck of the Edmund Fitzgerald

The legend lives on from the Chippewa on down
of the big lake they call "Gitche Gumee."
The lake it is said, never gives up her dead
when the skies of November turn gloomy.
With a load of iron ore twenty-six thousand tons more
than the Edmund Fitzgerald weighed empty,
that good ship true was a bone to be chewed
when the "Gales of November" came early.
The ship was the pride of the American side
coming back from some mill in Wisconsin.
As the big freighters go it was bigger than most
with a crew and good captain well seasoned,
concluding some terms with a couple of steel firms
when they left fully loaded for Cleveland.
And later that night when the ship's bell rang,
could it be the north wind they'd been feelin'?

The wind in the wires made a tattle tale sound
and a wave broke over the railing.
And every man knew as the captain did too
'twas the witch of November come stealin'.
The dawn came late and the breakfast had to wait
when the Gales of November came slashin'.
When afternoon came it was freezin' rain
in the face of a hurricane west wind.
When suppertime came the old cook came on deck
sayin', "Fellas, it's too rough t' feed ya."
At seven P.M. a main hatchway caved in;
he said, "Fellas it's been good t' know ya!"
The captain wired in he had water comin' in
and the good ship and crew was in peril.
And later that night when 'is lights went outta sight
came the wreck of the Edmund Fitzgerald.

Does anyone know where the love of God goes
when the waves turn the minutes to hours?
The searchers all say they'd have made Whitefish Bay
if they'd put fifteen more miles behind 'er.
They might have split up or they might have capsized;
they may have broke deep and took water.
And all that remains is the faces and the names
of the wives and the sons and the daughters.
Lake Huron rolls, Superior sings
in the rooms of her ice water mansion.
Old Michigan steams like a young man's dreams;
the islands and bays are for sportsmen.
And farther below Lake Ontario
takes in what Lake Erie can send her,
and the iron boats go as the mariners all know
with the Gales of November remembered.

In a musty old hall in Detroit they prayed,
in the "Maritime Sailors' Cathedral."
The church bell chimed 'til it rang twenty-nine times
for each man on the Edmund Fitzgerald.
The legend lives on from the Chippewa on down
of the big lake they called "Gitche Gumee."
"Superior," they said, "never gives up her dead
when the Gales of November come early!"

*Words and music by*
*Gordon Lightfoot*

Now that you have read *"The Wreck of the Edmund Fitzgerald,"* see if you can write the sequence of the details in prose. Is your prose statement as interesting as the song? Why or why not?

# Things to Do

Locate as many tapes or records of ballads as possible. Try to get song sheets that show you the words in print as well. Read the words to each ballad. Then listen to them. Compare the effectiveness of each ballad as it is read and as it is heard.

Study the ballads carefully and see how they relate the details of whatever they are describing. Then look at the meter and rhyme scheme of each.

Now it's time to try to write your own ballad. Select an event, a person, or an issue. You don't have to plan or write the music unless you want to. Just try to write the words. Perhaps you or a friend could strum a guitar as you read your ballad aloud.

## Narrative Poetry

A narrative poem, like a folk ballad, tells a story. However, a narrative poem is often more fully developed. Do you remember the characteristics of a short story? There is a definite plot structure—introduction, rising action, climax, falling action. There is a setting (time and place), a point of view (first or third person) and characterization. Narrative poetry has these characteristics too, even though it usually doesn't develop them as fully.

Here's a famous narrative poem. As you read it, see if you can visualize the action. When you get done, see if you can jot the details down in prose.

*The shadow of a cornstalk on the ground is lovely, but it is no denial of its loveliness to see as one looks on it that it is telling the time of day, the position of the earth and the sun, the size of our planet and its shape, and perhaps even the length of its life and ours among the stars.*

Arthur Miller

## The Charge of the Light Brigade

Half a league, half a league,
Half a league onward,
All in the valley of Death
   Rode the six hundred.
"Forward the Light Brigade!
Charge for the gun!" he said.
Into the valley of Death
   Rode the six hundred.

"Forward, the Light Brigade!"
Was there a man dismayed?
Not though the soldier knew
   Someone had blundered.
Theirs not to make reply,
Theirs not to reason why,
Theirs but to do and die.
Into the valley of Death
   Rode the six hundred.

Flashed all their sabers bare,
Flashed as they turned in air
Sabring the gunners there,
Charging, an army, while
    All the world wondered.
Plunged in the battery-smoke
Right through the line they broke;
Cossack and Russian
Reeled from the saber-stroke
    Shattered and sundered.
Then they rode back, but not,
    Not the six hundred.

Cannon to right of them,
Cannon to left of them,
Cannon behind them
    Volleyed and thundered;
Stormed at with shot and shell,
While horse and hero fell,

They that had fought so well
Came through the jaws of Death,
Back from the mouth of hell,
All that was left of them,
    Left of six hundred.

When can their glory fade?
O the wild charge they made!
    All the world wondered.
Honor the charge they made!
Honor the Light Brigade,
    Noble six hundred.

*Alfred, Lord Tennyson*

# Chapter 14

## "...With Thought and Feeling"

Do you recognize this instrument? The ancient Greeks used it much as we might use a folk guitar today. This instrument is called a lyre. It was first used to accompany the singing of songs or the telling of narrative poems, which were usually long epic tales of gods and superheroes. From the word lyre comes the term lyric, and a type of verse called lyric poetry. Like the old epics and ballads, lyric poetry is meant to be sung, but its purpose is not to tell a story. Its purpose is to convey thought and feeling. An increased emphasis on sound and rhythm usually is used to accomplish this purpose. This emphasis on sound and rhythm is easily recognized in vocal lyrics which are accompanied by musical instruments (from a guitar to a full orchestra).

The techniques used in lyric poetry that does not use musical accompaniment are more subtle. The words alone must convey the sounds and rhythms without the aid of musical instruments.

## Song Lyrics

Here are two songs by Rod McKuen, a contemporary poet and song writer. Although the author has set these lyrics to music, read them first as lyric poetry without any musical accompaniment.

## I've Saved the Summer

*by Rod McKuen*

I've saved the summer
and I give it all to you
to hold on winter morning
when the snow is new.

I've saved some sunlight
if you should ever need
a place away from darkness
where your mind can feed.

And for myself I've kept your smile
when you were but nineteen,
till you're older you'll not know
what brave young smiles can mean.

I know no answers
to help you on your way
the answers lie somewhere
at the bottom of the day.

But if you've a need for love
I'll give you all I own
it might help you down the road
till you've found your own.

# Some of Them Fall

### *by Rod McKuen*

Some of them fall like snowflakes
in the winter chill.
Some of them fall with no sound at all
and just roll down the hill.

Some of them fall like acorns
in the forest dense,
strung on a line of steel so fine
that makes a barbed-wire fence.

And some of their names are Eddie
and some of their names are Joe;
I can't say why some of them die. . .
that's not for me to know.

What are the elements of each of these poems that help convey the feeling? Notice the use of rhyme and meter. Can you picture these words being sung along with a guitar?

Perhaps you can locate Rod McKuen's recording of each of these. If so, listen to each one and compare the impact of the words as songs set to music with the power of these words as lyric poems that must stand on their own.

## Things to Do

Listen to as many song lyrics as you can. Select songs that have words which can stand on their own as lyric poetry. Try more Rod McKuen. Simon and Garfunkel and Bob Dylan are also good choices. Hard rock is less suitable for this purpose because of the power of the rhythm of the instruments, which completely overwhelms the words. Listen to songs and then try to read the lyrics as poems. Are there any which you like better as poems? Which ones absolutely need music to be effective?

Try writing some of your own lyrics. You don't have to set them to music. Just try to find words that really get across feelings or thoughts.

# Lyric Poetry

Here's a sonnet by Edna St. Vincent-Millay. These are not song lyrics, but an example of lyric poetry. Read this poem carefully and then try reading it aloud. See how the sounds and rhythm help convey feeling.

I shall go back again to the bleak shore
And build a little shanty on the sand,
In such a way that the extremest band
Of brittle seaweed will escape my door
But by a yard or two; and nevermore
Shall I return to take you by the hand;
I shall be gone to what I understand,
And happier than I ever was before.
The love that stood a moment in your eyes,
The words that lay a moment on your tongue,
Are one with all that in a moment dies,
A little under-said and over-sung.
But I shall find the sullen rocks and skies
Unchanged from what they were when I was young.

Emily Dickinson's poetry employs images so vivid, so unusual, that it conveys an extreme intensity of feeling. Her use of rhyme and meter is, like her imagery, quite unconventional. Here are three poems by Dickinson. Read them several times.

We play at Paste—
Till qualified, for Pearl—
Then, drop the Paste—
And deem ourself a fool—

The Shapes—though—were similar—
And our new Hands
Learned *Gem*-Tactics—
Practicing *Sands*—

I'll tell you how the Sun rose—
A Ribbon at a time—
The Steeples swam in Amethyst—
The news, like Squirrels, ran—
The Hills untied their Bonnets—
The Bobolinks—begun—
Then I said softly to myself—
"That must have been the Sun"!
But how he set—I know not—
There seemed a purple stile
That little Yellow boys and girls
Were climbing all the while—
Till when they reached the other side,
A Dominie in Gray—
Put gently up the evening Bars—
And led the flock away—


Should you but fail at—Sea—
In sight of me—
Or doomed lie—
Next Sun—to die—
Or rap—at Paradise—unheard
I'd *harass God*
Until he let you in!


Discuss these poems with a friend or in class. Take note of the imagery, especially in "I'll tell you how the sun rose."

Read the last of these three out loud again. How does the meter in the last two lines help to convey and emphasize what the poet is saying?

## Things to Do

Read as many lyric poems as you can. Dickinson, Shelley, Longfellow, Elizabeth Barrett Browning, Tennyson, are a few of the authors you might look at. Your teacher will suggest others.

When the spirit moves you, write some lyric poetry of your own. At first stick to the conventions. Use rhyme and meter in the more conventional ways to help you get the feelings across. And, if the spirit doesn't move you, try to write a poem anyway. You may surprise yourself.

## Free Verse

Now read this poem by Walt Whitman.

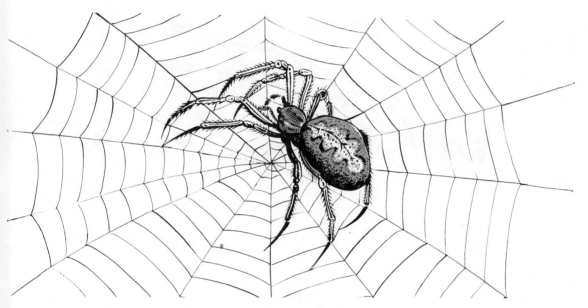

## A Noiseless Patient Spider

A noiseless patient spider,
I mark'd where on a little promontory it stood isolated,
Mark'd how to explore the vacant vast surrounding,
It launch'd forth filament, filament, filament, out of itself,
Ever unreeling them, ever tirelessly speeding them.

And you O my soul where you stand,
Surrounded, detached, in measureless oceans of space,
Ceaselessly musing, venturing, throwing, seeking the spheres to
    connect them,
Till the bridge you will need be form'd, till the ductile anchor hold,
Till the gossamer thread you fling catch somewhere, O my soul.

*Walt Whitman*

This poem illustrates a type of lyric poetry called free verse. Free verse doesn't rhyme and doesn't have a set meter. Its rhythmic patterns make it different from prose, but the rhythms are not prescribed as they are in the conventions of certain other kinds of poetry.

In reading and writing free verse, pay special attention to the rhythms created through line length and syllables within lines. Notice how the rhythm conveys meaning.

## The Red Wheelbarrow

so much depends
upon

a red wheel
barrow

glazed with rain
water

beside the white
chickens

*William Carlos Williams*

Look at each pair of lines in "*The Red Wheelbarrow*." Read the lines out loud and see how the rhythm is affected by line length and the pattern of syllables within lines.

Note the contrasting lengths of lines and the actual placement of the words. What effect would couplets of identical lengths have on the rhythm? Would the poem convey its meaning as effectively? Why or why not?

## Found Poetry: An Extreme Form of Free Verse

Free verse breaks many poetic conventions. Sometimes it breaks so many that it is very close to prose. Sometimes free verse can even be found in prose. When this happens, the result is frequently referred to as *"found"* poetry. Here are two examples of found poetry. Both of the following poems were found as advertisements, the first from a toy manufacturer, and the second in a film catalog for materials in basic geometry.

## Barbie Doll Goes to College

Now Barbie's
a co-ed!
Easy-to-assemble
college
includes
Dormitory,
Sweet Shoppe,
Stadium,
Drive-In Movie
and campus scenes,
plus exciting
furnishings
and accessories.
All in sturdy,
colorful
chipboard.
Compact, with
convenient
carrying handle.
Folds
neatly
away.

*Ronald Gross (b. 1935)*

# Adolescence

*Basic Geometry:*

Trisecting a straight line with triangles
Bisecting a straight line with triangles
Bisecting a straight line with compass
Drawing perpendicular and intersecting lines with triangles
Dividing an angle
Tangents
Tangent Problem 1
Tangent Problem 2
Tangent Problem 3
Tangent Problem 4
Tangent Problem 5
Tangent Problem 6
Tangent Problem 7
Drawing curved parallel lines

*E. J. Heiman*

# Things to Do

Take a metered rhymed lyric poem you have written. Work with it and modify the poetic conventions so that it becomes free verse. Be prepared to defend each modification as enhancing meaning.

It you can't bear to tamper with one of your own lyric poems, try the above activity with someone else's. You still have to defend your modifications.

*"Find"* some found poetry. Arrange it on a page to get the message across. Share it with your friends. Places to look might include the ads, both classified and others, in your newspaper. The real estate ads are often quite good. Look at the labels and directions on common household products.

Keep writing. When a poem happens, get it down on paper before it's gone. Don't be discouraged if you don't become a great poet overnight. As Emily Dickinson said, *"The truth must dazzle gradually, or else every man be blind."*

# INDEX